THE ESSENTIAL DOGEN

THE ESSENTIAL DOGEN

Writings of the Great Zen Master

Edited by
Kazuaki Tanahashi and Peter Levitt

SHAMBHALA
Boulder 2013

Shambhala Publications, Inc.
2129 13th Street
Boulder, Colorado 80302
www.shambhala.com

Quotations from *Moon in a Dewdrop*, edited by Kazuaki Tanahashi, published by North Point Press—ten poems plus four passages as indicated in the sources and translation credits—reprinted with permission by Farrar, Straus & Giroux.
Excerpt of fifteen lines from "Song" from *Collected Poems 1947–1980* by Allen Ginsberg. Copyright © 1954 by Allen Ginsberg. Reprinted by permission of HarperCollins Publishers and, in the United Kingdom, by permission of The Wylie Agency (UK) Limited.

14 13 12 11 10 9 8 7

Printed in the United States of America

Shambhala Publications makes every effort to print on acid-free, recycled paper.
Shambhala Publications is distributed worldwide by Penguin Random House, Inc., and its subsidiaries.

Designed by Daniel Urban-Brown

LIBRARY OF CONGRESS CATALOGING-IN-PUBLICATION DATA

Dogen, 1200–1253.
[Works. Selections. English]
The essential Dogen: writings of the great zen master /
edited by Kazuaki Tanahashi and Peter Levitt.—First edition.
pages cm
Includes bibliographical references.
ISBN 978-1-61180-041-8 (pbk.: alk. paper)
1. Zen Buddhism. I. Tanahashi, Kazuaki, 1933–. II. Levitt, Peter. III. Title.
BQ9449.D653E55 2013
294.3'927—DC23
2012037078

For Shirley and Linda
love and deep gratitude

Contents

PRACTICAL INSTRUCTION

HISTORY

GATES OF DHARMA

PHILOSOPHICAL VIEW

STUDENTS AND TEACHERS

EXPRESSION

Preface and Acknowledgments

Eihei Dogen (1200–1253) is one of the greatest elucidators of meditation in the ancient world. His writings today inspire many of those who contemplate in different spiritual traditions and are interested in expanding and deepening their meditative experience.

Dogen was an extraordinary thinker, visionary, poet, writer, scholar, teacher, introducer of Zen, leader of a spiritual community, and reformer of Buddhism in Japan. He is emerging as one of the most widely read and studied Buddhists in the Western world; more than sixty books in English with his name on their covers are available now. Yet his writings are often technical, paradoxical, enigmatic, and repetitive.

This volume is intended to make his writings easily accessible to readers, including those who are not familiar with Zen or Buddhism in general. Peter Levitt and I have selected passages from Dogen's enormous body of work throughout his career and classified them according to theme. We hope that this approach will help those who are interested in his thinking and teachings on various topics. We have also included a selection of Dogen's poems that, at a glance, might appear eccentric or absurd but may be more easily understood when placed in the context of his other writings.

Dogen was ordained as a monk at age fourteen (in the East Asian way of counting; see Editors' Notes to the Reader, page xxxix), started studying Zen at age eighteen, and went to China to complete his study between the ages of twenty-four and twenty-eight. He established his first training center, Kosho Monastery, when he was thirty-four and started building a full-scale monastery in a remote province of Echizen at age forty-four, which was established in the following year. He died at age fifty-four.

Treasury of the True Dharma Eye (*Shobo Genzo*) is Dogen's lifework. It is one of the first Buddhist teachings written in Japanese, in a mixture of ideographs and phonetics. Until then, Buddhists in his country had written their teachings in Chinese, which were then read in a Japanized Chinese manner. Dogen kept to the tradition of using Chinese when he quoted scriptures and earlier Zen stories. Most of our excerpts are from the book of the same title published recently by Shambhala Publications.

Dogen wrote two types of poems—*waka* and Chinese-style poems. Waka is an old style of Japanese poetry consisting of thirty-one syllables: five, seven, five, seven, and seven. Poems translated here in five lines are waka. The Chinese-style poems are found in another massive collection of Dogen's formal talks, monastic guidelines, and other types of talks and writings compiled by his senior students. *Dogen's Extensive Record: Translation of the Eihei Koroku* by Taigen Dan Leighton and Shohaku Okumura is an excellent presentation of this collection of Dogen's writings. We cross-reference the Chinese-style poems included in our book to the Leighton-Okumura book for comparison and to give the reader a sense of where these poems were placed in the original collection.

The Essential Dogen is the fifth of the San Francisco Zen Center's Dogen book projects—following *Moon in a Dewdrop*, *Enlightenment Unfolds*, *Beyond Thinking*, and *Treasury of the True Dharma Eye*. I deeply appreciate my thirty-six years of collaboration and friendship with all the staff and abbots of the Zen Center. My special gratitude goes to Michael Wenger, in charge of publication, for his continuous support and good ideas. I would like to thank all of my cotranslators of Dogen texts whose names are shown in the section "Sources and Translation Credits" for their great contribution.

Dogen is fortunate to have Peter Levitt, an accomplished Zen teacher, and outstanding poet, to help refine his expressions in the English language. Peter and I have been friends since 1987 and have worked together on a number of writing projects, including the last Dogen book, *Treasury of the True Dharma Eye: Zen Master Dogen's Shobo Genzo*. My annual visits to him in British Columbia, Canada, as well as his visits to Linda and me in Berkeley, California, are always full of tremendous pleasure. I thank Shirley Graham, his wife, a wonderful poet, for her kindness and support. My gratitude goes to Taigen Dan Leighton for his assistance on our selected bibliography. I also thank Lisa Senauke and Asaki Watanabe for their assistance on the "Sources and Translation Credits" section.

As always, it has been a great pleasure working with the Shambhala Publications staff. Peter and I thank Jonathan Green, Hazel Bercholz, and Ben Gleason. We appreciate DeAnna Satre for her copyediting. Our special appreciation goes to Dave O'Neal, our principal editor, who has guided us through the publication process.

—KAZUAKI TANAHASHI

A Walk with Dogen into Our Time

In 1954 poet Allen Ginsberg wrote a poem called "Song" that acknowledges the weight of our human circumstance and suffering in a particular and somewhat unusual way. I believe it may also provide a gateway to the following writings by Zen Master Eihei Dogen, who addressed the nature of reality as he came to understand the world of people and things through his lifetime practice of Zen.

As the poem begins, Ginsberg says:

> Under the burden
>   of solitude,
> under the burden
>   of dissatisfaction
>
>   the weight,
> the weight we carry
>   is love.

Suffering under such a weight is often accompanied by longing, as the poet well knew, and so his poem expresses the longing to return to that human possibility known by many names, including *wholeness, oneness, unity,* and *Self,* though Ginsberg simply called it *love.*

Quite young when the poem was written, the poet was inspired by an intuitive certainty that the twin burdens of solitude and dissatisfaction would be relieved if the realization of wholeness or love might find full expression in the world.

Of course, Ginsberg also understood that his longing for completion was not his alone but part of the common spiritual yearning experienced by people in every place and time, and so he acknowledges this in the final lines through the repetition of a single affirmative word, followed by other rhythmic phrasing that functions like the beating of a heart:

yes, yes,
        that's what
I wanted,
        I always wanted,
I always wanted,
        to return
to the body
        where I was born

The body of wholeness. The body of unity. What Zen monk Dogen called "the body after the final body," and what the poet identifies as the body of love. It is for this body he longed, and whatever words are used to point to the primordial condition of oneness acknowledged by virtually every spiritual tradition, Ginsberg importantly refers to the journey there as a "return."

More than seven hundred years before this poem was written, Dogen crossed the sea from Japan to China, following his sincere aspiration to realize wholeness, which, interestingly, he later referred to as a "return to the source," "return to reality," or "self returning to self," prefiguring Ginsberg's use of the word *return*. One of Dogen's primary motivations for making this dangerous journey was to study with authentic teachers so that he might satisfy his spiritual quest to fully realize "the great matter of birth-and-death."

After two years of significant study with other teachers, Dogen was told, "The only person in Great Song China who has a dharma eye is Old Man Rujing." Having also heard that Rujing would accept new students if they vowed to maintain the tradition of genuine, rigorous practice under his strict guidance, Dogen made his way to Rujing's temple.

Once at the Tiantong Monastery, he wrote to Rujing as "a humble person from a remote country" and requested permission to enter Rujing's inner chamber and receive the abbot's personal instruction. Rujing must have found the heartfelt authenticity of this request from a monk who had traveled so far in search of dharma quite compelling, for without ever having laid eyes on Dogen, he replied, "Yes, you can come informally to ask questions any time, day or night, from now on. Do not worry about formality; we can be like father and son." And he signed it, "Old man at Mount Taibo."

Rujing must also have perceived fire in the aspiration and practice of monk Dogen, whose own "Rules for Zazen" admonishes students of the way to be mindful of time's swift passage and "engage yourself in zazen as though saving your head from fire." At their very first meeting, when Dogen was twenty-six years old (in the East Asian way of counting), Rujing acknowledged him and said, "The dharma gate of face-to-face transmission from buddha to buddha, ancestor to ancestor, is actualized now."

Dogen began practice under Rujing's unwavering eye, and not long after, Rujing confirmed that Dogen had, indeed, "dropped away body and mind" and come to the great realization of wholeness for which Ginsberg would also long, in a place and time that even Dogen could not imagine.

For two more years, Dogen trained below Taibo Peak, whereupon Rujing acknowledged him as his dharma successor and presented him with the traditional document of heritage. Thereafter, Dogen returned to Japan, feeling the heavy burden on his shoulders "to spread the teaching and save sentient beings." True, his own sincere quest was satisfied, but now he pondered how he might nourish others' aspirations with the great care that had helped him to "return to the source."

Dogen certainly knew the profundity of one's aspiration to realize wholeness, and so he felt the pressing need to "leave for students of the way the authentic teaching of the buddha house." His deepest wish was to articulate both the principle and the path as Rujing had transmitted them to him, so that others might come to full understanding as well.

The depth of Dogen's compassion for others, and his commitment to provide authentic teachings, can be seen in an extraordinary essay written in 1231. As with much of Dogen's writing, "On the Endeavor of the Way" is alternately considered insightful and compelling or confusing and confounding by various readers, but Kazuaki Tanahashi, coeditor of this book, has noted it is "highly respected in the Soto School as Dogen's most comprehensive explanation of dharma."

In its entirety, this essay introduces primary themes Dogen would develop over his lifetime, while serving as a masterful clarification of wholehearted seated meditation (zazen), which Dogen refers to as "the authentic gate to free yourself." It also voices the burden he felt and the weight of love that the Ginsberg poem brings forward. Here is an excerpt from near the beginning:

> There may be true students who are not concerned with fame and gain, who allow their aspiration for enlightenment to guide them and earnestly desire to practice the buddha way. They may be misguided by incapable teachers and obstructed from the correct understanding; intoxicated in confusion they may sink into the realm of delusion for a long time. How can they nourish the correct seed of prajna and encounter the time of attaining the way? Since I am wandering about, which mountain or river can they call on? Because of my concern for them, I would like to record the standards of Zen monasteries that I personally saw and heard in Great Song, as well as the profound principle that has been transmitted by my master.

And so, having come to great realization under Rujing's guidance, Dogen understood fully in body and mind that from the very beginning, wholeness is the fundamental reality for all beings; that, in fact, every form of life is an all-inclusive manifestation of what might be called "original wholeness," though we suffer from the ingrained pattern of dualistic thinking that prevents us from knowing our complete and original self. As a result, Dogen initiated a lifetime of teaching and writing in one of the most unique and provocative styles the world has seen, so that others might also clarify the great matter of birth-and-death; self might have a bridge to self; wholeness in human form might be expressed as wholeness; and sentient beings might be saved from the unforgiving rigors of delusion, anguish, and needless suffering—*the burden of dissatisfaction*—in all of its forms.

During his lifetime, Dogen elucidated the principle and path of what I've called "original wholeness," a phrase I hope will join others in these comments to identify in contemporary speech what is usually referred to in more traditional Zen terminology. As the literature of Zen makes clear, it is difficult, if not impossible, for words and phrases to embody the true content and nature of realization. Brilliant and provocative as his words were, even Dogen's attempt to convey to Rujing the moment of his realization by saying "I have dropped away body and mind" may well have fallen short of the challenge to express his realization as it was in itself.

Our attempt to authentically communicate the subjective, ineffable experience (or *nonexperience*, as Dogen might say) of realization is hindered by the limiting ability of the very words we use. It was not Dogen's, and it is not anyone else's lack that the vivid power of experience cannot be fully embodied in words. No matter how compelling or beautiful they may be, words appeal in the main to the linear, thinking mind that thinks in words. Elegant, discerning, and seemingly endless in its capacity to comprehend, ultimately the cognitive faculty can only provide a partial understanding, since it is but one of the ways human beings "know" life as it occurs. There is still the intuitive to be considered, the physical, the dream. All of these and more are also authentic ways of knowing.

As a master of language, Dogen's usage was penetrating and poetic in the extreme. Well aware of its limitations, he developed a mode of expression to convey dharma that engages more of the human capacity for understanding than just the thinking mind, though certainly, as when he was at pains to meticulously describe the practice of meditation or provide temple guidelines, his writing was prescriptive and clear. Many of the practices found in Zen communities today are performed almost exactly as Dogen described.

When it came to a nuanced expression of dharma, however, he spun words and turned phrases constantly, often creating new meanings on the spot or using the same words and phrasing to make a point in the first moment and then contradict that very point in the next. His teachings, on occasion delivered past midnight during intensive periods of practice, might even be seen as a kind of linguistic acrobatics—a compelling, clarifying, and often confusing explosion of sentences that rely on subtlety, invention, piercing insight, and realized expression to embody his meaning and help students fulfill their deepest aspirations.

Filled with images, metaphor, logic and illogic, in addition to stories taken from the storehouse of the Buddha's teaching and the literature of Zen, which he would present in a manner that often overturned traditional interpretations, Dogen's teachings almost make a poetic and holographic impression in the body-mind that leaves a visceral impact while simultaneously appealing to the intellect. In so doing, he turns the body, turns the mind.

In one teaching that addresses the inherent qualites of words, Dogen's statement seems to undo everything I have been saying about the impossibility of using words to express enlightenment. As Kaz Tanahashi observes in his insightful translation of Dogen's lifework, *Treasury of the True Dharma Eye*, with regard to Zen Master Xiangyan's statement that "a painted rice cake does not satisfy hunger":

> This is usually interpreted as "studying words and letters does not help one to realize ultimate truth." Dogen's interpretation is that words and letters as an expression of enlightenment cannot be separated from the ultimate truth. Thus, "painted rice cake" means an expression of enlightenment.

I can only laugh. Quite a few times in the ten years of working with Kaz on our various Dogen projects (which has been a personal treasure and a source of great joy in my life), I would turn from the text and ask, "How in the world did he come up with this?" We could only shake our heads with appreciation for the depth of his understanding. "It's Dogen."

Dogen's use of what he called "intimate language," like the words and turning phrases of the buddha ancestors who came before him, is rooted in the nondual experience of realization. It is intended to help students yield the grip of linear, discriminative thinking and turn the mind toward an understanding of things as they truly are. Creative and virtuosic in this regard, he may be Zen's greatest precontemporary postmodern decon-structionist elucidator of the way.

Dogen's teachings were offered to women and men, lay and monastic alike (though of course the primary recipients were his monastic students), with the expectation that they would work in conjunction with the primary activity of those who studied the buddha way: the steadfast practice of zazen. They were intended as companions of this activity, a wake-up stick whose touch and sound might resound deeply in a student's awakening field of understanding. They were never meant to replace seated meditation or to provide linguistic entertainment for students to spin in their minds while sitting idly on their cushions.

Challenging as these teachings were, Dogen's use of words to undo words and his twirling of concepts to unravel concepts helped students to embrace his instruction to study them *intimately*—his credo in all things—until the lock of discriminative thinking fell away and their practice deepened to where thinking "beyond thinking" became the activity of zazen itself.

Dogen points in this direction in his essay "The Point of Zazen":

Yaoshan, Great Master Hongdao, was sitting. A monk asked him, "In steadfast sitting, what do you think?"
   Yaoshan said, "Think not-thinking."
   "How do you think not thinking."
   Yaoshan replied, "Beyond thinking."

And in "On the Endeavor of the Way," Dogen encouraged his students in the following manner:

Sit zazen wholeheartedly, conform to the buddha form, and let go of all things. Then, leaping beyond the boundary of delusion and enlightenment, free from the paths of ordinary and sacred, unconstrained by ordinary thinking, immediately wander at ease, enriched with great enlightenment. When you practice in this way, how can those who are concerned with the traps and snares of words and letters be compared to you?

The ability to leap beyond dualistic thinking during zazen is fundamental to Dogen Zen. It is due to the wholehearted, all-inclusive nature of the activity, but we should look at this carefully to be sure we discern his meaning. As taught by Dogen, meditation does not lead to enlightenment. In fact, there is no distance of any kind between meditation and enlightenment. There is not even a separation between one's aspiration to realize the self and that very realization. According to Dogen, from the very first moment of establishing the meditation posture, no bridge is necessary; practice *is* full realization, and full realization *is* practice. As he says, "Between aspiration, practice, enlightenment, and nirvana, there is not a moment's gap."

Dogen's understanding is that at all moments we are whole, lacking nothing despite how we may feel at any given time. Therefore, zazen is not a practice that leads to realization. It is neither a means to an end in our usual goal-oriented manner of thinking nor a method for learning to concentrate; nor is it a technique designed to help us improve ourselves, though the practice may help to bring some of that about.

Dogen's teaching is clear: zazen is "the dharma gate of enjoyment and ease," an intimate expression of the oneness of all life as it manifests in human form. It is realization itself, whether we are aware of it or not. It confirms what has traditionally been called "original self" or, more provocatively, "your face before your parents were born." And so we do not sit in order to become enlightened; we sit as an expression of enlightenment. That is what buddhas do.

Of course, Dogen knew that students might greet this lofty teaching with doubt, as some Zen practitioners today will verify, and so he addressed the issue directly:

> Know that fundamentally you do not lack unsurpassed enlightenment; you are replete with it continuously. But you may not realize it and may be in the habit of arousing discriminatory views and regarding them as real.

To clarify his teaching on the inseparability of practice and enlightenment, Dogen used the Japanese word *shusho*, the equivalent of the English term *practice-enlightenment*, or *practice-realization*. He relied on teachings such as the following to bring his point across:

> One time, Huineng, Old Buddha of Caoxi, asked a monk, "Do you depend upon practice and enlightenment?"
> The monk replied, "It's not that there is no practice and no enlightenment. It's just that it's not possible to divide them."
> This being so, know that the undividedness of practice and enlightenment is itself the buddha ancestors.

But just to sweeten the pot, here is another statement Dogen made on what he called "the thunderstorm of the buddha ancestors' samadhi." I imagine it is one his students had to swallow whole during zazen in order for it to blossom in their lives. "Enlightenment," he wrote, "actualizes buddha nature through practice."

While for Dogen all beings are "fundamentally enlightened," it is reasonable to ask, as he did during his travels in China: If this is the case and we are whole from the beginningless beginning, why do we practice? To answer, I'd like to offer a response based on Dogen's teaching: We practice because we do not yet know who or what we are. But as a result of many causes, including the suffering we experience and the longing engendered by that suffering, we aspire to know. That aspiration leads many people to begin the practice of zazen.

Dogen expressed this beautifully when he said, "Wisdom is seeking wisdom." Perhaps we might paraphrase and say that wholeness is seeking wholeness, self is seeking self.

Dogen's understanding of original wholeness is a radical and life-giving affirmation of all being, where the word *radical* means "root." At first it may be difficult for us to hear what he is saying. After all, most of us were raised with the idea inherited from our various religious traditions that originally we are not at one with Oneness, that from the moment of conception we live at a distance from the source of life. Except for the more mystical orientation within these traditions that speaks of immanence, divinity is seen as solely transcendent and, thereby, is considered "radically other" from human beings.

This belief in distance and otherness is a powerful root of the culturally pervasive view that consciously and unconsciously shapes our lives. As such, it affects how we experience who and what we are. In addition, the fracturing pressures of contemporary life might lead many of us to agree that we live at a distance not only from the source but also from ourselves.

In saying this, I am reminded of a comment made by Franz Kafka, who wrote with such accuracy, pathos, and humor about the bizarre and dislocating minefield of modern society. When asked about his connection to others particular to his ethnic and religious community, he replied, "What do I have in common with them? I hardly have anything in common with myself!"

I don't believe Kafka is alone in feeling at odds with himself. Contemporary people trying to get through the overburdened scatter of a day could easily agree. And Dogen might well have been looking directly at us through time when he wrote, "Your thoughts run around like a wild horse, and your feelings jump about like a monkey in the forest." Given this disposition and the increasing pace and unpredictability of life as we edge further into the twenty-first century, it's no wonder we experience such a pervasive sense of anxiety and dislocation.

But there is more. Just as our religious traditions affect our understanding, the defining influence of secular and cultural values has a considerable effect as well. In our culture, this includes the glorification of the rugged individualist, an idea that reifies and seems to concretize the separateness of each person, who, according to the mythology, must confront life and nature alone and stand in isolated opposition to all others in order to survive. Is this not part of what creates the burden of solitude to which Ginsberg referred?

In addition, there is the societal expectation of endless acquisition whose underlying message that what we are and what we have are not enough epitomizes the burden of dissatisfaction. Though many have found ways to keep the more insatiable appetites at bay, the acquisitive sensibility keeps the mind of comparison, judgment, envy, and greed spinning. Sadly, no realm of life remains immune, including the realm of spiritual aspiration and practice.

What a far cry this is from Dogen's realization of wholeness, or even the occasional experience of feeling at one with ourselves, with life, and with the world. The suffering produced by these powerful influences undermines our sense of wholeness and denies the reality of the interdependent fabric of life that brings all things into existence and makes them what they are.

Although what is now called interdependence, which Dogen understood as basic to buddha dharma, is widely accepted as an accurate description of life functioning exactly as it does, the belief in eternal separation continues to have a devastating effect on our personal lives and world. In the most extreme cases, it rationalizes the poison of aggressive actions against those we identify as "other," promoting racism, sexism, the decimation of the natural world, and war.

Caught in the grip of such discriminative thinking, there is no room for us to experience intimacy. And yet intimacy, especially as Dogen understood it, is a primary antidote to many of the causes of destruction that, in part, define our age.

The Japanese words Dogen used to express "intimate" are *shimmitsu* or *shinsetsu*. For Dogen, "intimate means close and inseparable. There is no gap. Intimacy embraces buddha ancestors. It embraces you. It embraces the self. It embraces action. It embraces generations. It embraces merit. It embraces intimacy."

When speaking of an experience, as when Dogen exhorts students to make an intimate study of the self, the ideograph carries the sense of being both all-inclusive, or all-encompassing, and immediate. Practicing seated meditation in a way that embodies all-inclusive immediacy is what Dogen meant by "engage yourself in zazen as though saving your head from fire."

It is worth noting that a principal definition of the ideographs Dogen used to express wholeness, *ichinyo* in Japanese, is also "inseparable," with the literal meaning of "one thusness" driving the sense of what *inseparable* means. According to Kaz Tanahashi, "one thusness" may be understood to mean "not one, not two" or "oneness," so there is the clear implication of all-inclusiveness here as well. Nothing left out, no gap.

"Intimacy" then, means nondual. It is another word for original wholeness. To clarify the point so that there is no confusion: the fact of oneness does not imply that we do not have personal lives, each with individual attributes. Oneness does not deny individuality in any form; it makes it possible. Without the nondual functioning of oneness, nothing could exist. And without each thing existing and functioning exactly as it does, oneness cannot be manifested. As Dogen wrote on the subject of practice-realization, and as the teaching on form and emptiness found in the *Heart Sutra* (a central text of Mahayana Buddhism, including Zen) makes clear, "not one, not two" means "it is not possible to divide them."

For Dogen, intimacy is life itself. If we "study this intimately," as he instructed his students to do, we may gain some insight into what he means when using terms like *intimate realization, intimate life.* Whether or not we practice daily meditation, we might take Dogen's exemplification of intimacy in the form of zazen to mean that while intimacy certainly includes being or feeling close to someone, intimacy does not stop there. Dogen's use of the word means holding nothing back while giving ourselves completely to the only moment in which we are. In this way the moment (time) and what we are doing in that moment (being) are one intimate expression of life. Dogen calls this "time being" in one of his most beautiful and intricate teachings.

There is the undeniable demand of thoroughness here, a quality of being best described as through-and-through, one hundred percent; a way of using ourselves fully so that we merge with our activity and, in so doing, merge intimately with all things. Dogen's teaching that "to master one dharma [to be intimate with one thing] is to master all dharmas" points right at all-encompassing thoroughness as one of the hallmarks of intimacy.

It is true, of course, that Dogen spoke of intimacy and what I've called original wholeness within the strict context of Zen as it was practiced in medieval Japan, but the reach and importance of these teachings are not limited by the circumstances in which they were first given. For Dogen, the centrality of zazen cannot be separated from his great realization, and while it may be anathema to some to suggest that his teachings can be applied outside a contemporary version of that context, at this historical time there is a need for the life-giving potential these teachings provide. Therefore, it may be beneficial to look within our daily lives to find ways to embrace Dogen's vision, his understanding, and whatever practices we can on behalf of ourselves, our families, society, and the world at large.

For those who do practice zazen, or who might like to establish a meditation practice, Dogen offers encouragement and guidance. In addition to the instructions he provides in "Rules for Zazen," in the fascicle "King of Samadhis," in *Treasury of the True Dharma Eye*, he writes, "Like the sun illuminating and refreshing the world, this sitting removes obscurities from the mind and lightens the body so that exhaustion is set aside." It is a perfect prescription for the exhausting travail of our too-busy lives.

Furthermore, he says, when we "gather together all distracted thought and scattered mind within this posture," zazen "keeps your heart and mind from being stirred." It is no small thing to have a touchstone practice every day that allows "the monkey and horse to step back and reflect on themselves" so we can experience clarity and the calming of disturbing emotions. This does not mean that we do not feel deeply or are somehow able to avoid the external or internal conditions that usually cause great upset—far from it, since Dogen taught that we should make an all-encompassing effort to meet our life as it comes to us without reservation. But it does mean that in our meditation practice, "when you are fully present, you are free of how broad or narrow it is where you are."

The ability to be fully present yet not controlled by conditions creates a stable mental and emotional foundation even in the midst of turmoil. It is a natural ability each of us has, and the benefit of establishing this greater stability can be quite significant for every aspect of our lives. If we practice it, Dogen tells us, it is realized, or "made real," from the first moment we sit down until beyond the last, so the motivation to practice with consistency arises from the practice itself.

Dogen's realization of oneness as it appears in all of its diverse expressions reflects the field of life itself. It has been described as an open field, boundless, with a gateless gate through which to enter. It is the field in which compassion grows naturally because the usual barrier between "self" and "other" is seen through and no longer blocks the way. As Kaz Tanahashi has noted, "Only when we identify ourselves with others can we genuinely act with love toward others."

In order to effectively express the connection and compassion we feel, however, our actions must be practical and in accord with actual, everyday life. If we remain in the realm of nonduality, or if we are attached to the ephemeral realm of ideas alone, the ability to actualize wholeness will remain beyond our grasp. As Kaz wrote, "An enlightened person is someone who embodies the deep understanding of nonduality while acting in accordance with ordinary boundaries, not being bound to either realm but acting freely and harmoniously." I find this a perfect description of the phrase "not one, not two," which reflects the disposition of mind found in Dogen's teaching.

It was with this orientation that we gathered and organized the excerpts for this book, to serve as possible gateways for readers so that Dogen's wisdom might touch their lives in a way that brings them closer to themselves and all things. As we read through the material from which we chose our selections, we saw that Dogen's teaching on wholeness offers a positive, life-loving principle and path for people in our time to engage the very same questions humans have always faced: the impermanence of life and the great matter of birth-and-death; the fact of suffering; the undeniable chain of cause and effect; and how in the midst of life's greatest difficulties, we can meet life with a mind that is "joyful, kind, and great" so we can still "nourish the sacred body" of all things and discover how the miracle of each moment can be experienced with our whole heart and mind.

In a brief teaching titled "Undivided Activity," which Dogen gave to an assembly of laypeople in Kyoto in 1242, he underscored the importance of each person's living a full and active life, reminding them that "your understanding can be manifested moment after moment." Given what we know of Dogen's own understanding, perhaps we can say that his hope was to encourage listeners to "fully actualize life" in every possible way.

Toward the end of his life, Dogen prepared a rough draft on an ancient Buddhist treatise called *One Hundred Eight Gates of Realizing Dharma*. The treatise emphasized the importance of using skillful means in order to realize dharma all the way through. Though Dogen's notes are scant, here are a few examples from the treatise itself:

Pure practice of mind is a gate of realizing dharma; it keeps the mind from the three types of poison [greed, aggression, and ignorance of oneness]. . . . Compassion is a gate of realizing dharma; it encompasses wholesome roots in all realms of birth. . . . Mindfulness of giving is a gate of realizing dharma; it makes you free from wanting a reward. . . . Right skillful means is a gate of realizing dharma; it embodies right action.

As readers will see, the gateways in the pages of this book reflect these one hundred eight gates in various ways. Some of the gateways may prove more easily entered than others, but that is a common feature of living. After reading Dogen's writing and contemplating how to enter dharma gates skillfully so that life in its wholeness is actualized right where we are, we might come up with our own list and approach. Some readers may feel inspired to practice Zen or establish a meditation practice and might seek out a teacher or community where this can be done. Others may determine that they would like to increase personal awareness when in the grip of difficult or provocative emotions that reinforce the burden of solitude and may therefore choose mindfulness practice as a gate. Since one gate opens onto another, mindfulness often leads to the gate of compassion and acceptance without a moment's gap.

Readers who are committed to addressing social or environmental issues with greater awareness and compassion, despite being up against difficult circumstances and aggressive opponents, will find many gates here. I know one man who realized that he relied on anger while working to help protect life in the ocean. From what he said, ever since childhood he intuitively followed Dogen's teaching to "look after water and grain with compassionate care, as if tending your own children," and yet his actions as an adult were so tied to rage that he contributed to the very violence he opposed. When he realized that he was actually tearing at the fabric of oneness he believed he was working to sustain, he stepped through the gate of dropping self-righteous thinking and behavior and made a radical shift that affected every aspect of his life.

Finally, because there is no end to the need for the dharma gate of skillful means, another gate to consider is Dogen's reminder that whatever we do has an effect quite particularly attached to its causation, so that before we act we consider its effect broadly for the near term and the far. This teaching on karma provides a gate of compassionate attention that can easily be applied to speech, livelihood, personal relationships, service, and actions of every kind.

In closing this introduction, I'd like to step away from speaking about gates and offer a window into some of the text you are about to read. In the context of studying Dogen with others over the years, one thing has become clear: We cannot, of course, know with any precision what Dogen may have had in mind when writing some of the more intricate or perplexing teachings that rely on his great realization. But it is right in those moments, when we do not understand, that it may benefit us to remember that he is always trying to help us realize our own wholeness, our oneness, ourselves. If in those moments of confusion we look again and remember Dogen's aspiration in teaching as he did, it may prove of some use in the end.

Kaz and I have gratefully walked with Dogen as one of life's great teachers and companions for many years. Our hope is that readers may draw close and discover him to be a true companion as well.

—PETER LEVITT
SALT SPRING ISLAND, BRITISH COLUMBIA

Editors' Notes to the Reader

SOURCES

The majority of excerpts in this book are from four Dogen books edited by Kazuaki Tanahashi and one book translated by him with John Daido Loori. The prose and poems are slightly revised. We also provide our new translations of some poems by Dogen. The sources and translation credits are presented at the end of the main part of the book.

DOGEN'S LIFE

A detailed chronology of Dogen's life based on textual evidence is presented in the back of this book.

NOTES

Translators' interpolations are presented in brackets in the main text. Words and phrases with asterisks are briefly explained in the endnotes.

TRANSLITERATION

Chinese terms are represented by the Pinyin system.

ENGLISH APPROXIMATIONS

CHINESE	ENGLISH
c	ts
q	ch
x	sh

Macrons for Japanese words are used only in the endnotes and in the chronology of Dogen's life.

The letter *g* in Dogen's name is pronounced as in *gate* rather than *gentle*.

NAMES

The abbots of Zen monasteries are often called by the name of the mountain, monastery, or region where they resided. Monasteries themselves are sometimes represented by the names of the mountains they are on.

DATES

This book follows the lunar calendar, used traditionally in East Asia. The first to third months correspond to spring, and the other seasons follow in three-month periods. The fifteenth day of the month is the day of the full moon. (An intercalary month was occasionally added to make up a year.) The years are in the solar calendar.

AGE

This book follows the traditional East Asian way of counting ages, where a person is one year old at birth and gains a year on New Year's Day. That means Dogen was one year old in 1200, and died at age fifty-four in 1253.

PRACTICAL INSTRUCTION

Aspiration and Search

"Aspiration for enlightenment" is called "hotsu bodai shin" in Japanese, or in short, "hosshin." It is sometimes translated as "beginner's mind." "Way-seeking mind" (doshin) is another name for it (in this case, way means enlightenment). Dogen describes his motivation for seeking authentic buddha dharma and offers his insightful views on aspiration—one of the central elements of Buddhist practice.

———————————

I wrote to Master Rujing* shortly before I met him: "When I was young I aroused the aspiration for enlightenment and visited various monasteries in my country. I had some understanding of the principle of cause and effect; however I was not able to clarify the real source of buddha,* dharma,* and sangha.* I was only seeing the outer forms, the marks, and the names. Later I entered the chamber of Eisai,* Zen Master Senko, and for the first time heard the teaching of the Linji School.*

"Now I have accompanied Monk Myozen* to the flourishing kingdom of Song China.* After a voyage of many miles, during which I entrusted my phantom body to the billowing waves, I have finally arrived and have entered your dharma assembly. This is the fortunate result of my wholesome roots from the past.

"Great compassionate teacher, even though I am only a humble person from a remote country, I am asking permission to be a room-entering student, able to come to ask questions freely and informally. Impermanent and swift, birth-and-death is the issue of utmost urgency. Time does not wait for us. Once a moment is gone, it will never come back again, and we're bound to be full of regret.

"Great compassionate reverend abbot, grant me permission to ask you about the way, about the dharma. Please, I bow to you one hundred times with my forehead humbly touching the floor."

Rujing wrote back: "Yes, you can come informally to ask questions any time, day or night, from now on. Do not worry about formality; we can be like father and son." And he signed it, "Old Man at Mount Taibo."

—

The aspiration for enlightenment arouses itself. This arousing is the aspiration for enlightenment. The aspiration for enlightenment is neither existent nor nonexistent, neither wholesome, unwholesome, nor neutral. It is not the result of past actions. Even beings in the blissful realms can arouse it. The aspiration for enlightenment arises just at the time of arising; it is not limited by conditions.

—

From the moment of arousing the aspiration for enlightenment, you take steps on the journey in the endeavor of the way. Merging with realization and thorough understanding are all the vital eye, bones, and marrow that dash into seeing the Buddha.* This being so, the total world of self, the total direction of other, this and that are all the practice of seeing the Buddha.

⸻

You should stop searching for phrases and chasing after words. Take the backward step and turn the light inward. Your body-mind of itself will drop off and your original face will appear. If you want to attain just this, immediately practice just this.

⸻

Endeavor wholeheartedly to follow the path of earlier sages. You may have to climb mountains and cross oceans when you look for a teacher to inquire about the way. Look for a teacher and search for understanding with all-encompassing effort as if you were coming down from heaven or emerging from the ground. When you encounter the teacher, you invoke sentient beings as well as insentient beings. You hear with the body, you hear with the mind.

⸻

To arouse the aspiration for enlightenment is to make an offering of sand or rice water to the Buddha. It is to make an offering of a handful of food to sentient beings. It is to make an offering of a bouquet of flowers to the Buddha. To practice a small virtuous act with the encouragement of someone else, or to bow to the Buddha following a demon's deceptive advice, is also arousing the aspiration for enlightenment.

⸻

In general, when you are a beginner, you cannot fathom the buddha way. Your assumptions do not hit the mark. The fact that you cannot fathom the buddha way as a beginner means not that you lack ultimate understanding but that you do not recognize the deepest point.

⸺

Eighty thousand skandhas [all phenomena] become the causes and conditions for arousing the aspiration for enlightenment. There are those who arouse the aspiration for enlightenment in a dream and attain the way. There are those who arouse the aspiration for enlightenment and attain the way while intoxicated. There are those who attain the way when they see flowers flying or leaves falling. Others attain the way among peach blossoms or green bamboo. Some attain the way in a deva* realm or in the ocean. They all attain the way.

⸺

As soon as you arouse aspiration for enlightenment, even if you transmigrate in the six realms and four forms of birth, transmigration itself will be your practice of enlightenment. Although you may have wasted time so far, you should vow immediately, before this present life ends: "Together with all sentient beings, may I hear the true dharma from this birth on throughout future births."

⸺

To study with mind means to study with various aspects of mind, such as consciousness, emotion, and intellect. After resonating with the way and arousing the aspiration for enlightenment, take refuge in the great way of buddha ancestors* and devote yourself to the practice of way-seeking mind. Even if you have not yet aroused the way-seeking mind, follow the examples of buddha ancestors who did arouse the way-seeking mind in former times.

⸺

Awake or Asleep

Awake or asleep
in a grass hut,
I pray
to bring others across
before myself.

Zazen

Zazen is a Japanese word that means "meditation in a sitting posture." The word zen, *meaning "meditation," derives from the Sanskrit word dhyana and its Chinese transliteration channa, which is abbreviated as chan. This type of meditation is the central activity in the Chan or Zen School as well as an important practice in other schools of Buddhism.*

This ordinary everyday sitting is itself boundless joy.

To transcend the world directly, to manifest the magnificence of the buddha ancestors' house—this is sitting in the meditation posture. To leap over the heads of outsiders and demons and become a true person inside the buddha ancestors' room—this is sitting in the meditation posture. To sit in the meditation posture is to transcend the deepest and most intimate teaching of buddha ancestors. Thus, buddha ancestors practice this way without needing to do anything else.

Shakyamuni Buddha* said to the assembly, "When you sit in the meditation posture, you realize samadhi* in body and mind

8

and give rise to an awesome virtue that people respect. Like the sun illuminating and refreshing the world, this sitting removes obscurities from the mind and lightens the body so that exhaustion is set aside.

$$=$$

All buddha tathagatas* who individually transmit inconceivable dharma, actualizing unsurpassable, complete enlightenment, have a wondrous art, supreme and unconditioned. Receptive samadhi* is its mark; only buddhas transmit it to buddhas without veering off. Sitting upright, practicing Zen, is the authentic gate to free yourself in the unconfined realm of this samadhi.

$$=$$

Mazu* of Jiangxi practiced with Nanyue,* who intimately transmitted the mind seal to him. This was the beginning of polishing a tile. Living in the Chuanfa Temple, Mazu was engaged in the continuous practice of zazen for more than a decade. Ponder his sitting on a rainy night in a thatched-roof hut. There is no account that he skipped sitting on a cold platform when stranded by snow.

When Nanyue visited his hut, Mazu stood up.

Nanyue said, "What have you been doing these days?"

Mazu said, "I have been just sitting."

Nanyue said, "What is your intention in just sitting?"

Mazu said, "I intend to become a buddha."

Then Nanyue picked up a tile and started polishing it on a stone near Mazu's hut.

Mazu said, "Master, what are you doing?"

Nanyue said, "Polishing a tile."

Mazu said, "Why are you polishing the tile?"

Nanyue said, "I am trying to make a mirror."

Mazu said, "How can you polish a tile and make a mirror?"

Nanyue said, "How can you do zazen and become a buddha?"

Mazu said, "Then, how so?"

Nanyue said, "When driving a cart, if it stops moving, do you whip the cart or the ox?"

Mazu was silent.

⸺

Even if you obtain some ideas by studying koans* and words, it may cause you to go further away from the buddha ancestors' path. Instead, dedicate your time to sitting upright, not seeking achievement, and not seeking enlightenment. This is the ancestral way.

Although teachers of old used verbal studies along with just sitting, they were totally engaged in sitting. There were those whose enlightenment was revealed by verbal studies. But this was due to the strength of zazen. The true power lies in sitting.

⸺

Sit zazen wholeheartedly, conform to the buddha form, and let go of all things. Then, leaping beyond the boundary of delusion and enlightenment, free from the paths of ordinary and sacred, unconstrained by ordinary thinking, immediately wander at ease, enriched with great enlightenment.

⸺

RULES FOR ZAZEN

Practicing Zen is zazen. For zazen, a quiet place is suitable. Lay out a thick mat. Do not let in drafts or smoke, rain or dew. Protect and maintain the place that contains your body. There are examples from the past of sitting on a diamond seat and sitting on a flat stone covered with a thick layer of grass. Day or night, the place of sitting should not be dark; it should be kept warm in winter and cool in summer.

Set aside all involvements and let the myriad things rest. Zazen is not thinking of good, not thinking of bad. It is not conscious endeavor. It is not introspection. Do not desire to become a buddha. Let sitting or lying down drop away. Be moderate in eating and drinking. Mindful of the passing of time, engage yourself in zazen as though saving your head from fire. On Mount Huangmei,* Hongren,* the Fifth Ancestor, practiced zazen to the exclusion of all other activities.

When sitting zazen, wear the kashaya* and use a round cushion. The cushion should not be placed all the way under the legs but only under the buttocks. In this way the crossed legs rest on the [soft] mat and the backbone is supported by the round cushion. This is the method used by all buddha ancestors for zazen.

Sit either in the half-lotus position or in the full-lotus position. For the full-lotus put the right foot on the left thigh and the left foot on the right thigh. The toes should lie along the thighs, not extending beyond. For the half-lotus position, simply put the left foot on the right thigh.

Loosen your robes and arrange them in an orderly way. Place the right hand on the left foot and the left hand on the right hand, with the ends of the thumbs lightly touching each other. With the hands in this position, place them close to the body so that the joined thumb tips are at the navel.

Straighten your body and sit upright. Do not lean to the left or right; do not bend forward or backward. Your ears should be in line with your shoulders, and your nose in line with your navel.

Rest your tongue against the roof of your mouth and breathe through your nose. Lips and teeth should be closed. Eyes should be open, neither too wide nor too narrow. Having adjusted body and mind in this manner, take a breath and exhale fully.

Sit solidly in samadhi and think not thinking. How do you think not thinking? Beyond thinking. This is the art of zazen.

Zazen is not learning to do concentration. It is the dharma gate of great ease and joy. It is undivided practice-realization.

Samadhi

Samadhi is a Sanskrit word indicating the one-pointed state of body and mind in meditation (zazen). It is translated as ding in Chinese, which means "stability."

On Zazen Practice

The moon
abides in the midst
of serene mind;
billows break
into light.

⸺

The activity of zazen is just like the fish swimming. Who can measure how many thousands and myriads of miles there are in zazen? Its journey is the entire body going on the path where no bird flies.

⸺

The Tathagata, the World-Honored One,* taught his disciples how to sit and said to them, "If you want to manifest samadhi and enter it, you should gather together all distracted thought and scattered mind within this posture. Practice in this way and you will manifest and intimately enter the king of samadhis."

Thus we clearly know that sitting in the meditation posture is itself the king of samadhis. It is itself entering realization.

⸺

When even for a moment you sit upright in samadhi expressing the buddha mudra [form] in the three activities [body, speech, and thought], the whole world of phenomena becomes the buddha mudra and the entire sky turns into enlightenment. At this moment, all things actualize true awakening; myriad objects partake of the buddha body; and sitting upright, a glorious one under the bodhi tree,* you immediately leap beyond the boundary of awakening. Then you turn the unsurpassably great dharma wheel* and expound the profound wisdom, ultimate and unconditioned.

⸺

Honored practitioners of Zen, please do not grope for the elephant or try to grasp the true dragon. Strive to hit the mark by directly pointing. Revere the mind that goes beyond study and surpasses all doings. Experience the enlightenment of the buddhas, correctly inheriting the samadhi of the ancestors. Practice thusness* continuously and you will be thus. The treasury will open of itself for you to use as you wish.

⸺

In the great way of going beyond, no endeavor is complete without being one with myriad things. This is ocean mudra samadhi.* In ocean mudra samadhi, all elements are as they are. It is not that there is no practice and realization, it is just that they are not divided. This is called ocean mudra samadhi.

＝

Samadhi is to enter but not to come out. If you are not suspicious and fearful of a true dragon, you have no doubts to let go of at the very moment of seeing the Buddha.

＝

Here is the place; here the way unfolds. The boundary of realization is not distinct, for the realization comes forth simultaneously with the full experience of buddha dharma. Do not suppose that what you attain becomes your knowledge and is grasped by your intellect. Although actualized immediately, what is inconceivable may not be apparent. Its emergence is beyond your knowledge.

Bowing

Bowing with palms together expresses respect to the awakened nature of others. It also sanctifies and expresses gratitude to the room where one practices, the meditation seat, and anything that is offered, including food. Formal bowing follows an offering of incense and is done in multiple prostrations to the floor.

Bowing Formally

A snowy heron
on the snowfield
where winter grass is unseen
hides itself
in its own figure.

You abandon the household by realizing that your house is not a true house. You enter the mountain and practice dharma. You create a buddha image and build a stupa.* You chant a sutra and recite the Buddha's name. You look for a teacher and inquire about the way. You sit in meditation posture. You bow to the three treasures. You recite homage to the Buddha.

≈

To bow all the way to the floor and to bow standing are awesome presence in motion and stillness. Painting a decayed tree and polishing a brick of dead ash continues without stopping. Even though calendar days are short and urgent, study of the way in this manner is profound and deep.

≈

Rujing chanted a verse:

> Both the bower and the bowed-to
> are empty and serene by nature—
> the way flows freely between them.
> How wondrous!

≈

When the emperor bows to a monk or nun, the monk or nun does not bow back. When devas bow to monks and nuns, the monks and nuns do not bow back. This is because the merit of being a home leaver is excellent. If bowed to by home-leaver monks or nuns, the devas' palaces, radiant light, and the wholesome results of their actions immediately crash and fall apart.

≈

The great dharani [magic]* is a formal greeting. Because a formal greeting is a great dharani, you encounter the actualization of a formal greeting. The phrase "formal greeting" originated in China and has been widely used for a long time. It has not been transmitted by Indra* or from India but from buddha ancestors. It is not in the realm of sound or form. Do not wonder if it came from before or after the King of the Empty Eon.*

A formal greeting means burning incense and bowing. A root teacher is someone who has ordained you or has transmitted dharma to you. These two may be the same person. You stay with and see your root teacher. This is the dharani of making greetings. Be close to your teacher without long absences.

$$\approx$$

When bowing remains in the world, buddha dharma remains. When bowing disappears, buddha dharma disappears.

Each Activity Is Sacred

Mindfulness and a respectful heart in each moment are applied equally in meditation and other daily activities including work, interaction with others, and cleansing one's body. Practicing and living in this way helps us to clearly see, understand, and value what is right before us as none other than the wholeness of life itself. As Dogen says, even our eating bowls are the body and mind of buddha ancestors.

———————————

We will thoroughly engage in each activity in order to cultivate fertile conditions to transform the ten directions.

⹀

If there is sincerity in your cooking and associated activities, whatever you do will be an act of nourishing the sacred body. This is also the way of ease and joy for the great assembly.

⹀

In performing your duties along with the other officers and staff, you should maintain joyful mind, kind mind, and great mind.

⹀

When you prepare food, do not see with ordinary eyes and do not think with ordinary mind. Take up a blade of grass and construct a treasure king's land; enter into a particle of dust and turn the great dharma wheel. Do not arouse disdainful mind when you prepare a broth of wild grasses; do not arouse joyful mind when you prepare a fine cream soup. Where there is no discrimination, how can there be distaste? Thus, do not be careless even when you work with poor materials, and sustain your efforts even when you have excellent materials. Never change your attitude according to the materials. If you do, it is like varying your truth when speaking with different people; then you are not a practitioner of the way.

During my stay at Mount Tiantong, a priest named Yong from Qingyuan Prefecture held the position of tenzo [head cook]. One day after the midday meal when I was walking along the eastern covered walkway to a subtemple called Chaoran Hut, he was in front of the buddha hall drying some mushrooms in the sun. He had a bamboo stick in his hand and no hat on his head. The sun was very hot, scorching the pavement. It looked very painful; his backbone was bent like a bow and his eyebrows were as white as a crane.

I went up to the tenzo and asked, "How long have you been a monk?"

"Sixty-eight years," he replied.

"Why don't you let a helper do it?"

"Others are not myself."

"Reverend sir, you follow regulations exactly, but as the sun is so hot, why do you work so hard as this?"

"Until when should I wait?"

So I stopped talking. As I was walking farther along the covered walkway, I thought about how important the tenzo's position is.

—

The awesome practice inside the Buddha's washhouse is cleansing, which has been transmitted from ancestor to ancestor. That the buddha procedure is still being practiced is an auspicious joy for those who long for the ancient way. This is encountering what is rare to encounter.

When you wash in the true dharma authentically transmitted by buddhas and ancestors, the inside and outside of body and mind, as well as the inside, the outside, and the in-between of the five organs,* six sub-organs,* body, mind, environs, the world of phenomena, and empty space are immediately cleansed. When you cleanse with incense and flowers, the past, present, future, causes and conditions, actions and effects are immediately purified.

—

When Linji* was at the assembly of Huangbo,* he planted cedar and pine trees with Huangbo. Huangbo asked him, "Why are we planting so many trees deep in this mountain?"

Linji said, "First, for the landscape around the monastery. Second, as a landmark for later generations." Then he hit the ground twice with his hoe.

Huangbo held up his staff and said, "That's why I have just given you thirty blows."

Linji heaved a deep sigh.

Huangbo said, "When you receive my teaching, it will flourish in the world."

Robe

Three types of robes were among the few things monks and nuns were allowed to possess: the outer robe, the inner robe, and the great robe. The kashaya, which covers one shoulder, functions as the symbol of home leavers.

Once when I was in Song China, practicing on a long sitting platform, I observed the monks around me. At the beginning of zazen in the morning, they would hold up their kashayas, place them on their heads, and chant a verse quietly with palms together:

> Great is the robe of liberation,
> the robe beyond form, the field of benefaction!
> I wear the Tathagata's teaching
> to awaken countless beings.

This was the first time I had seen the kashaya held up in this way and I rejoiced, tears wetting the collar of my robe. Although I had read this verse of veneration for the kashaya in the *Agama Sutra*,* I had not known the procedure. Now I saw it with my own eyes. In my joy I also felt sorry that there had been no master to teach this to me and no good friend to recommend it in Japan. How sad that so much time had been wasted! But I also rejoiced in my wholesome past actions [that caused me to experience this]. If I had stayed in my land, how could I have sat side by side with the monks who had received and were wearing the buddha robe? My sadness and joy brought endless tears.

Then I made a vow to myself: However unsuited I may be, I will become an authentic holder of the buddha dharma, receiving authentic transmission of the true dharma, and with compassion show the buddha ancestors' authentically transmitted dharma robes to those in my land.

Know that a kashaya is the buddha body, buddha mind. It is called a robe of emancipation, a field of benefaction. It is called a robe of patience, a robe beyond form. It is called a robe of compassion, a robe of the Tathagata, a robe of unsurpassable, complete enlightenment. Receive and maintain it accordingly.

If you make patched robes and mend bowls your whole life, build a thatch-roofed hut near a mossy cliff or white rock, and practice sitting upright, you immediately go beyond buddha and directly master the great matter of your life's study.

With this body and capacity, you transform the ordinary and enter the sacred. With this effect and reward, you go beyond buddha and beyond ancestor. Through this cause and condition, you pick up dirt and turn it into gold. Through this effect and reward, there is transmission of dharma and entrustment of the robe.

Once your body is wrapped in a kashaya, you attain Shakyamuni Buddha's flesh, hands and feet, head and eyes, marrow and brains, radiant light, and turning of the wheel of dharma. You wear a kashaya in this way. This actualizes the power of the robe. You vow and make offerings to Shakyamuni Buddha by maintaining, enjoying, protecting, and wearing the kashaya. By doing so, the practice of countless eons is thoroughly experienced.

HISTORY

Vulture Peak

The story of the Buddha holding up a flower and transmitting dharma to Mahakashyapa* on Vulture Peak in the kingdom of Magadha, northeastern India, is traditionally used to establish the authenticity of dharma in the Zen School. Hence, Mahakashyapa is regarded as its First Ancestor. This story is often considered the root of what is known as face-to-face or mind-to-mind transmission in Zen.

Once, on Vulture Peak in India, in the midst of a vast assembly of beings, Shakyamuni Buddha held up an udumbara blossom and blinked. Mahakashyapa smiled. Then Shakyamuni Buddha said, "I have the treasury of the true dharma eye, the wondrous heart of nirvana.* I entrust it to Mahakashyapa."

This is the meaning of transmitting the treasury of the true dharma eye, face-to-face, from buddha to buddha, from ancestor to ancestor. It was authentically transmitted through the Seven Original Buddhas* to Mahakashyapa. From Mahakashyapa there were twenty-eight transmissions up to and including Bodhidharma.* Venerable Bodhidharma himself went to

China and gave face-to-face transmission to Huike, Great Master Zhengzong Pujue. There were five transmissions through [the Sixth Chinese Ancestor] Huineng,* Great Master Dajian of Mount Caoxi. Then there were seventeen transmissions through Rujing, my late master, Old Buddha Tiantong of the renowned Mount Taibo, Qingyuan Prefecture, Great Song.

———

Within three, four, five, or six blossoms is within countless blossoms. Blossoms embody deep, vast characteristics of inside and reveal high and vast characteristics of outside. This outside-inside is the blooming of one blossom. Because there is just one branch, there are no other branches, no other trees. Every place reached by one branch is right now This is Old Man Gautama.* Because it is just one branch, it is entrusting, heir to heir.

This being so, "I have the treasury of the true dharma eye. This is entrusted to Mahakashyapa" and "You have attained my marrow." This realization everywhere leaves nothing that is not deeply revered. Thus, five petals open; the five petals are plum blossoms.

———

Mountains, rivers, sun, moon, wind, and rain, as well as humans, animals, grass, and trees—each and all have been held up. This is holding up the flower. The coming and going of birth and death is a variety of blossoms and their colors. For us to study in this way is holding up the blossom.

Bodhidharma

Bodhidharma is regarded as the Twenty-eighth Indian Ancestor and the First Chinese Ancestor of the Zen School. Legend has it that he journeyed across the sea from India to China and landed at the southern kingdom of Liang.

Bodhidharma went to the capital city of Jinling* and met with Wu,* who said, "Ever since I became Emperor, I have built temples, copied sutras, and approved the ordination of more monks than I can count. What is the merit of having done all of this?"

Bodhidharma said, "There is no merit."

The Emperor said, "Why is that so?"

Bodhidharma said, "These are minor achievements of humans and devas, which become the causes of desire. They are like shadows of forms and not real."

The Emperor said, "What is real merit?"

Bodhidharma said, "When pure wisdom is complete, the essence is empty and serene. Such merit cannot be attained through worldly actions."

The Emperor said, "What is the foremost sacred truth?"
Bodhidharma said, "Vast emptiness, nothing sacred."
The Emperor said, "Who is it that faces me?"
Bodhidharma said, "I don't know."

The Emperor did not understand. Bodhidharma knew that there was no merging [between the two of them] and the time was not ripe. Thus, without a word he left on the nineteenth day of the tenth month [of 527 C.E.] and traveled north of the River Yangzi.

He arrived in Luoyang* in the Kingdom of Wei on the twenty-third day of the eleventh month of the same year. He stayed at the Shaolin Temple of Mount Song,* where he sat facing the wall in silence day after day. But Emperor [Xiaoming] of Wei* was unaware of his presence and was not ashamed of being unaware of it.

—

In China after the Later Han Dynasty [25–220 C.E.], the teachings of Buddhist scriptures were introduced and spread all over the land, but there was no conclusive teaching as yet. When Bodhidharma came from India, the root of twining vines was immediately cut off and the pure, single buddha dharma spread. Hope that it will be like this in our country.

—

Finally Huike* reached Bodhidharma's dwelling but was not allowed to enter. Bodhidharma did not turn around. Throughout the night Huike did not sleep, sit, or rest. He stood firmly until dawn. The night snow seemed to have no mercy, piling higher and burying him up to his waist. Every drop of his tears froze. Seeing his frozen tears, he shed even more tears. Looking at his own body, he thought to himself, "A seeker in the past crushed his bones, extracted his marrow, and squeezed his blood to feed the starving people. Another seeker laid down his hair on the muddy road to let the Buddha pass. Another threw his body off the cliff to feed a tiger. They were like that. Then who am I?" Thus, his aspiration became stronger.

Those who study nowadays should not forget Huike's words, "They were like that. Then who am I?" If we forget, we will drown for numberless kalpas. Thus Huike addressed himself in this way, strengthening his aspiration for dharma. He did not mind being covered by snow. When we imagine the hair-raising ordeal of that long night, we are struck with terror.

At dawn Bodhidharma took notice and asked, "What do you seek? Why have you stood in the snow for so long?"

Shedding more tears, Huike said, "All I wish is that you compassionately open the gate of sweet dew in order to awaken many beings."

Bodhidharma said, "The unsurpassed, inconceivable way of all buddhas must be practiced hard and consistently for vast kalpas. You must bear what is unbearable. But if you wish with small virtue, small wisdom, and casual, arrogant mind for the true vehicle, you will toil in vain."

Then Huike was encouraged. Unnoticed by Bodhidharma, he took a sharp knife, cut off his left arm, and offered it to him.

Bodhidharma knew then that Huike was a dharma vessel and said, "When buddhas first seek the way, they give up bodily form for the sake of dharma. Now that I see your determination, you are invited to pursue the way here."

Thus Huike entered Bodhidharma's inner chamber, attending to him with great diligence for eight years. Huike was indeed an example and a great guide for humans and devas to follow. Such great diligence had not been heard of either in India or in China. When it comes to "smiling," you should study Mahakashyapa. And when it comes to attaining the marrow, you should study Huike.

———

Bodhidharma once said to his students, "The time has come. Can you express your understanding?"

Then one of the students, Daofu, said, "My present view is that we should neither be attached to letters nor be apart from letters and allow the way to function freely."

Bodhidharma said, "You have attained my skin."

The nun Zongchi said, "My view is that it is like the joy of seeing Akshobhya Buddha's* land just once and not again."

Bodhidharma said, "You have attained my flesh."

Daoyu said, "The four great elements are originally empty and the five skandhas* do not exist. Therefore, I see nothing to be attained."

Bodhidharma said, "You have attained my bones."

Finally, Huike bowed three times, stood up, and returned to where he was.

Bodhidharma said, "You have attained my marrow." Thus he confirmed Huike as the Second Ancestor and transmitted dharma and the robe to him.

———

When Bodhidharma gives transmission, he is Bodhidharma. When the Second Ancestor attains the marrow, he is Bodhidharma. Because people have studied the meaning of this, buddha dharma has continued to be buddha dharma to this day. If they had not studied, buddha dharma would not have reached to this day. Quietly pursue and investigate the meaning of this point for yourself and others.

Once Bodhidharma said to Huike, "If you put all the outside conditions to rest, your mind will not be agitated. With your mind like a wall, you will enter enlightenment."

Huike spoke of mind, spoke of essence in various ways, yet could not merge with realization for a long time. But one day he got it all of a sudden. So he said to Bodhidharma, "Now I have put all the conditions to rest for the first time."

Knowing that Huike had realization, Bodhidharma did not push him further. He only said, "Have you attained annihilation?"

Huike said, "No, I haven't."

Bodhidharma said, "What is your experience?"

Huike said, "It is always so clear that I cannot explain it."

Bodhidharma said, "This is the essential mind transmitted by all buddhas and ancestors from the past. You have now attained it. Maintain it well."

⸻

Xiangyan,* Great Master Xideng of the Xiangyan Monastery, whose priest name was Zhixian, was a dharma heir of Guishan.*

He once said to the assembly, "What if you are hanging by your teeth from a branch in a tree on a one-thousand-foot cliff, with no place for your hands or feet to reach? All of a sudden someone under the tree asks you, 'What is the meaning of Bodhidharma coming from India?' If you open your mouth to respond, you will lose your life. If you don't respond, you don't attend to the question. Tell me. What would you do?"

Then senior monk Zhao* from Hutou came out and said, "Master, I will not ask you about being in a tree. But tell me, what happens before climbing the tree?"

Xiangyan burst into laughter.

Let me ask the old gimlets [seasoned practitioners] throughout past and present: When Xiangyan burst into laughter, is it speaking in the tree or speaking under the tree? Is it or is it not responding to the question: What is the meaning of Bodhidharma coming from India? Tell me, how do you see it?

⸺

Spring Snow Night

Snowdrifts like those in the old days at Shaolin.
Whole sky, whole earth, whole spring—new.
Inheriting the robe, attaining the marrow—to join the
  ancestors,
who would avoid standing in snow through the night?

Scriptures

The intellectual understanding of words in Buddhist sutras may not lead to one's direct realization. On the other hand, scriptures are a primary source of Buddhist teachings. Dogen ponders this dilemma.

In China, since the time Bodhidharma, the Twenty-eighth Ancestor, came from India, the principle that there is dharma heritage in the buddha way has been authentically understood. Before that time, it had never been spoken of. Although teachers of scriptures or treatises have received a human body as a vessel of the way, they are uselessly entangled by the net of scriptures; they do not understand the method of breaking through and cannot realize the moment of leaping out.

A monk called Fada* visited the assembly of Huineng, Zen Master Dajian of the Baolin Monastery, Mount Caoxi, Shao Region, Guangdong, Tang China. He boasted that he had chanted the *Lotus Sutra**three thousand times.

Huineng said to him, "Even if you have chanted the sutra ten thousand times, if you don't understand the meaning of it, you won't even know your own errors."

Fada said, "Because I am stupid, I have only been able to follow the words and chant. How can I understand the meaning of it?"

Huineng said, "Chant it for me. I will elucidate its meaning for you."

Fada chanted the sutra.

At chapter 2, "Skillful Means," Huineng said, "Stop. The essential meaning of this sutra is the causes of the Buddha's emergence into the world. Many parables are expounded, but there is nothing more than this. This cause is the single essential matter. What is the single essential matter? It is the buddha unfolding knowledge and entering realization. You are originally buddha knowledge. You who have this knowledge are a buddha. You should trust right now that the buddha knowledge is your own mind."

Then he taught with a verse:

When your mind is deluded, you are turned by the dharma
    blossoms.
When your mind is enlightened, you turn the dharma
    blossoms.
If you cannot clarify the meaning after chanting the sutra
    at great length, you become its enemy.
Thinking beyond thinking is right.
Thinking about thinking is wrong.
If thinking and beyond thinking do not divide the mind,
    you can steer the white-ox cart endlessly.

The meaning of studying sutras is that if you understand and follow the rules of practice for sudden or gradual realization taught by the Buddha, you will unmistakably attain enlightenment. In studying sutras you should not expend thoughts in the vain hope that they will be helpful for attaining realization.

〰

Even one thousand sutras and ten thousand attainments cannot match one realization.

〰

Buddha ancestors all expound sutras. What expounds sutras is empty space [boundlessness]. Without being empty space, no one can expound even one single sutra. Expounding the *Heart Sutra**and expounding the body sutra are both done with empty space.

〰

Zhaozhou,* Great Master Zhenji of the Guanyin Monastery, Zhao Region, was once given a donation by an old woman and was asked to rotate [chant] the canon.

He got off the meditation platform, walked around it, and said to the messenger, "The canon has been rotated."

The messenger went back to the old woman and reported this. The old woman said, "I asked the master to rotate the entire canon. Why did he only rotate half of the canon?"

〰

There are no voices or forms that are more beneficial than buddha sutras. Voices and forms delude you, and yet you tend to seek them and be greedy for them. On the other hand, buddha sutras do not delude you. Do not slander them with a lack of trust in them.

〰

Both following a teacher and following a sutra are following yourself. A sutra is no other than a sutra as yourself.

≈

You receive sutras and expound sutras by means of mountains, rivers, and earth or by means of the sun, the moon, and the stars. Likewise, you hold sutras and transmit sutras with the self before the Empty Eon, or with body and mind before the original face. You actualize such sutras by cracking open particles. You bring forth such sutras by cracking open the world of phenomena.

≈

Arousing the aspiration for enlightenment depends on sutras and teachers. Practice depends on sutras and teachers. The fruit of enlightenment is one and intimate with sutras and teachers.

≈

A sutra is the Tathagata's entire body. To bow to a sutra is to bow to the Tathagata's entire body. To encounter a sutra is to encounter the Tathagata's entire body.

≈

The sutras are the entire world of the ten directions. There is no moment or place that is not sutras. The sutras are written in letters of the supreme principle and of the secular principles. The sutras are written in letters of heavenly beings, human beings, animals, fighting spirits, one hundred grasses, or ten thousand trees. This being so, what is long, short, square, and round, as well as what is blue, yellow, red, and white, arrayed densely in the entire world of the ten directions, is no other than letters of the sutras and the surface of the sutras. Regard them as the instruments of the great way and as the sutras of the buddha house.

Schools of Zen

In China the Five Schools of Zen developed during the ninth century and thereafter. Many Zen teachers characterized their teaching as "directly pointing to the human mind, transmission outside the scripture." Thus the notion of direct experience "here and now," counter to scriptural studies, was often regarded as the identity of the Zen schools. Dogen criticizes this widespread tendency.

Rujing said, "The great road of buddha ancestors is not concerned with inside or outside. The reason they call it transmission outside the scripture is this: although Kashyapa Matanga* and others had transmitted the scriptural teaching to China previously, in coming here from India, Bodhidharma brought the teaching to life and showed the craft of the way. This is why they call it transmission outside the teaching. But there aren't two buddha dharmas. Before Bodhidharma arrived in China, there were practices but no master to enliven them. After Bodhidharma came to China, it was as if an aimless people acquired a strong king who brought the land, people, and property of the kingdom into order."

＝＝

Know that the buddha way, which has been transmitted from past buddhas, is not called Zen meditation, so how could there be the name "Zen School"? Clearly understand that it is an extreme mistake to use the name "Zen School."

＝＝

Bodhidharma went to China and entrusted dharma to the great master Huike; this was the beginning of dharma transmission in the eastern country. In this way, by direct transmission, it reached Huineng, the Sixth Ancestor, Zen Master Dajian. Then the authentic buddha dharma spread in China and the teaching that is not concerned with concepts and theories took form.

At that time there were two outstanding disciples of Huineng: Nanyue Huairang and Qingyuan Xingsi.* They both equally received the buddha's seal as guiding masters of humans and devas. Their two lineages spread, and later the Five Gates opened: the Fayan School,* the Guiyang School,* the Caodong School,* the Yunmen School,* and the Linji School. At present in Great Song China, only the Linji School prospers throughout the country. But in spite of their different styles, each of the Five Houses holds the one seal of the buddha mind.

＝＝

When the great master Bodhidharma sat facing the wall at the Shaolin Temple on Mount Song for nine years, neither monks nor laypeople knew the buddha's true teaching, so they called him the Brahman who concentrated on zazen. Subsequently, all buddha ancestors of every generation always devoted themselves to zazen. Heedless laypeople who saw them, without knowing the truth, informally called them the Zazen School. Later the word *za*—sitting—was dropped, and nowadays it is called the Zen School.

———

Rujing said, "In ancient times monasteries did not carry names like the Doctrinal School,* the Precept School,* or the Zen School. The use of such names is simply a bad habit of this declining age. Kings' officials who really do not know buddha dharma mistakenly classify monks as monks of the Doctrinal School, the Precept School, or the Zen School. Imperial tablets use these designations, and their usage has spread so that now we hear of five types of monks: Precept School monks, who are descendants of Nanshan;* Doctrinal School monks, who are descendants from the Tiantai;* monks of the Yoga School,* who are descendants of Amoghavajra;* monks of monasteries without lineages who are not clear about who their ancestors are; and the Zen monks, who are all descended from Bodhidharma. It is truly pitiful that we have such a confusion of names and groups in this remote country, China, in this declining age."

———

Before I formally bowed to Rujing, Old Buddha, I was trying to thoroughly study the profound teaching of the "Five Schools." But after I formally bowed to Rujing, I understood clearly that the "Five Schools" are groundlessly named.

In this way, when the buddha dharma was flourishing in China, there was no such designation as Five Schools, and there were no teachers of old to expound the teaching using the name of the Five Schools. After the buddha dharma became shallow and declined, the name Five Schools groundlessly appeared. This is because people have been negligent in study and not intimate in the endeavor of the way.

Authenticity

For Dogen the most crucial criterion for teaching, including his own, is authenticity, which consists of the direct experience of reality passed on from an awakened one to another, supported by scriptural teachings. Ironically, this experience is also described as "realization without a teacher and scripture." This phrase may be understood to mean no separation between the self and the teacher or scripture.

I would like to record the standards of Zen monasteries that I personally saw and heard in Great Song, as well as the profound principle that has been transmitted by my master. I wish to leave for students of the way the authentic teaching of the buddha house.

All those who study truth in buddha dharma in the past and present always investigate thoroughly with buddha ancestors to determine the authenticity of teaching from the past. They do not ask others for this. Those who are not authenticated by buddha ancestors are not buddha ancestors. Those who want to be authenticated should be authenticated by buddha ancestors. The reason is that the original teachers of mastering the dharma wheel are buddha ancestors.

⸺

Since a buddha receives dharma from a buddha, the buddha way is thoroughly experienced by a buddha and a buddha; there is no moment of the way without a buddha and a buddha.

⸺

Without being authentically transmitted heirs of buddha ancestors, you have not yet known the body-mind of buddha dharma. Without knowing the body-mind of buddha dharma, you have not yet clarified the buddha work. That the buddha dharma of Shakyamuni Buddha has spread throughout the ten directions means that the body-mind of the Buddha is actualized. The very moment of the body-mind of the Buddha being actualized is just this.

⸺

In the authentic tradition of our heritage, it is said that this directly transmitted, straightforward buddha dharma is the unsurpassable of the unsurpassable. From the first time you meet a master, without depending on incense offering, bowing, chanting buddha names, repentance, or reading scriptures, just wholeheartedly sit, and thus drop away body and mind.

⸺

Just understand that when a master who has attained the way with a clear mind authentically transmits to a student who has merged with realization, then the wondrous dharma of the Seven Original Buddhas, in its essence, is actualized and maintained. This cannot be known by those who study words. Therefore, set aside your doubt, practice zazen under an authentic teacher, and actualize buddhas' receptive samadhi.

Since authentic transmission is conducted from self to self, the self is within authentic transmission. You authentically inherit one mind from one mind. Thus there is one mind in authentic transmission.

It is taught that everyone attains the way by practice. Particularly in this authentically transmitted teaching of zazen, you are filled with the treasure you already have, entering dharma and leaving bondage behind. Those who practice know whether realization is attained or not, just as those who drink water know whether it is hot or cold.

When you first seek dharma, you imagine you are far away from its environs. At the moment when dharma is authentically transmitted, you are immediately your original self.

The mind that has been authentically transmitted is: one mind is all things, all things are one mind.

One who has attained dharma is a true authentic buddha and should not be regarded the same as before. When we see the person, someone who is new and extraordinary sees us. When we see the person, today sees today.

When you have the seal of realization from a buddha, you have realization without a teacher, realization without self.

GATES OF DHARMA

The Awakened Way

Dogen calls his path in everyday life "the awakened way" or "the buddha way" instead of "Zen" or "Zen School." It is the path of being a buddha, which is no other than going beyond buddha.

———————————

Endeavor in zazen is the straight path of the buddha way. Clarify the principle through sitting and seeing.

⹀

Without practice, the buddha way cannot be attained. Without study, it remains remote.

⹀

The body and mind of the buddha way is grass, trees, tiles, and pebbles, as well as wind, rain, water, and fire. To turn them around and make them the buddha way—this is the aspiration for enlightenment.

⹀

The buddha way is the buddha way even when you first arouse the aspiration for enlightenment. It is the buddha way when you attain authentic enlightenment. It is the buddha way altogether at the beginning, in the middle, and at the end. It is like journeying a long distance; one step is within one thousand miles, one thousand steps are within one thousand miles. The first step and the one-thousandth step are different but are equally within the one thousand miles.

—

Nanyue, who would later become Zen master Dahui, first went to meet Huineng, the Old Buddha of Caoxi. Huineng said, "What is it that thus comes?"

Nanyue studied this lump of mud all-inclusively for eight years and finally presented a move to Huineng: "I understand now. When I first came here, you instructed me: 'What is it that thus comes?'"

Then Huineng said, "How do you understand it?"

Nanyue said, "Speaking about it won't hit the mark."

This is the actualization of all-inclusive study, the realization of eight years.

Huineng said, "Does it depend on practice and realization?"

Nanyue said, "It is not that there is no practice and no realization, it is just that they cannot be divided."

Then Huineng said, "I am like this, you are like this, and all the buddha ancestors in India are also like this."

After this, Nanyue practiced all-inclusively for eight more years; counting from beginning to end, it was an all-inclusive study of fifteen years.*

—

Know that buddhas in the buddha way do not wait for awakening. Active buddhas alone fully experience the vital process on the path of going beyond buddha.

—

Practice just here is not apart from realization. Fortunately, each one of us has individually inherited this wondrous practice; each beginner's endeavor of the way brings forth original realization in the realm of the unconstructed.

Rujing said: "Let me explain this more clearly with an analogy. It is like a candle with its illuminating flame. When the candle is lit, there is a flame. As the candle burns, there is still the same flame. So there's no difference between the beginning time and the later time of the candle burning. The candle burns straight down, and it never burns backward. The flame is neither new nor old. Neither is it the possession of the candle nor does it exist apart from the candle. The flame is like the light of the beginner's mind. The candle, when it is flameless, is like the lack of vision of one who has not begun the way.

"The wisdom flame of the beginner's mind is complete at the outset. The all-inclusive samadhi of buddha ancestors is the completion of that same wisdom over time, burning down the confusion of ignorance till the candle is no more. Can you see how this practice has no beginning and no end, how now and later are not really different? This is the essential teaching correctly transmitted by buddha ancestors."

Enlightenment

Awakening to the ultimate reality of human existence is called "realization" or "enlightenment." It is the actualization of our innate capacity to experience wisdom beyond wisdom.

———————————

[According to Ejo*:] One day a student asked, "Although I have been studying the way for years, I haven't been enlightened. The teachers of old have said, 'Don't depend on intelligence and learning.' So I believe that even if I am slow and have little wisdom, I should not become discouraged. Is there anything to learn from the teachers of old about this?"

Dogen instructed, "You are right. Inherent intelligence or high capacity is not necessary. You should not depend on brilliance or smartness. Don't exclude those who are very slow or less talented. It is a mistake, however, to say that for the true study you should be like a blind, deaf, or mute person. The true study of the way should be easy. But even among hundreds and thousands of students in the assembly of one teacher in Great Song China, those who genuinely attain the way and inherit dharma are only one or two. Therefore, we should keep the examples of the ancient masters in mind.

"I see that there are those who have the utmost aspiration and those who don't. Those who have the utmost aspiration and study accordingly will not fail to attain the way. You should remember that how much you study and how fast you progress are secondary matters. The joyfully seeking mind is primary.

"Those who vow to steal a precious treasure, to defeat a powerful enemy, or to know a beautiful woman will follow their intention and keep it in mind on each occasion under all circumstances while walking, standing, sitting, and lying down. Nothing is left unachieved with such a commitment. If you seek the way with genuine intention as you practice just sitting, as you work on koans about ancient teachers, or as you face the teacher, then you can shoot a bird however high in the sky or catch a fish however deep in the water. But without arousing such a determined mind, how can you achieve the great matter of cutting off the transmigration of birth and death at the very moment the words *buddha way* are uttered? Those who have such a determined mind will invariably be enlightened, whether or not they are less learned or are slow, whether or not they are foolish or unwholesome.

"Upon arousing this mind, you should reflect on the impermanence of the world. Impermanence is not something you merely visualize or something you create and think about. Impermanence is the truth that is right in front of you. You need not study other people's words or textual evidence on this matter. To be born in the morning and to die in the evening, not to see someone today whom you saw yesterday—the impermanence of life is in your eyes and ears. You should not see or hear it only in terms of others but apply it to your own self.

"Even if you hope to live for seventy or eighty years, in the end you are destined to die. You should regard your pleasures and sorrows, relationships, and attachments in worldly affairs as your enemy. To do so is the way to a fuller life. You should keep in mind the buddha way alone and work for the bliss of nirvana. Especially those of you who are elderly or who are middle-aged, how many years do you have left? How can you be lax in your practice of the way?

"Yet this is not urgent enough. You should examine both the mundane world and the buddha realm. Tomorrow, or even in the next moment, you might become gravely ill, lose your senses, and suffer from great pain. You might be suddenly killed by a demon, a robber, or an enemy. Truly nothing is for certain. Therefore, in this transient world where the time of death is unpredictable, scheming to live forever or wasting your time plotting against others is quite stupid.

"The Buddhas spoke this truth to sentient beings. Ancestors expounded solely on this matter. I also speak of impermanence, the swift passage of time, and the urgency of birth and death. Do not ever forget this truth. Realize that you have just today, just this moment. You should concentrate your mind on the study of the way without wasting your time. If you do this, your practice becomes easy. To discuss the superiority or inferiority of your nature, or the brilliance or slowness of learning, is not necessary."

⸺

When you ride in a boat and watch the shore, you might assume that the shore is moving. But when you keep your eyes closely on the boat, you can see that the boat moves. Similarly, if you examine myriad things with a confused body and mind, you might suppose that your mind and essence are permanent. When you practice intimately and return to where you are, it will be clear that nothing at all has unchanging self.

—

Enlightenment and clarity of the mind occur only in response to the sustained effort of study and practice. Endeavoring in the way ripens the conditions of your practice. It is not that the sound of the bamboo is sharp or the color of the blossoms is vivid. Although the sound of the bamboo is wondrous, it is heard at the moment when it's hit by a pebble. Although the color of the blossoms is beautiful, they do not open by themselves but unfold in the light of springtime. Studying the way is like this. You attain the way when conditions come together. Although you have your own capacity, you practice the way with the combined strength of the community. So you should practice and search with one mind with others.

—

To study the way of enlightenment is to study the self. To study the self is to forget the self. To forget the self is to be actualized by myriad things. When actualized by myriad things, your body and mind as well as the bodies and minds of others drop away. No trace of enlightenment remains, and this no-trace continues endlessly.

—

If you attain unsurpassable, complete enlightenment, all sentient beings also attain it. The reason is that all sentient beings are aspects of enlightenment.

—

Enlightenment is like the moon reflected on the water. The moon does not get wet, nor is the water broken. Although its light is wide and great, the moon is reflected even in a puddle an inch wide. The whole moon and the entire sky are reflected in dewdrops on the grass or even in one drop of water.

Enlightenment does not divide you, just as the moon does not break the water. You cannot hinder enlightenment, just as a drop of water does not crush the moon in the sky. The depth of the drop is the height of the moon. Each reflection, however long or short its duration, manifests the vastness of the dewdrop and realizes the limitlessness of the moonlight in the sky.

═

All ancestors and all buddhas who uphold buddha dharma have made it the true path of unfolding enlightenment to sit upright, practicing in the midst of receptive samadhi. Those who attained enlightenment in India and China followed this way. Thus teachers and disciples intimately transmitted this excellent art as the essence of the teaching.

═

Within this unsurpassable manifestation of enlightenment, the entire world of the ten directions is but a small portion; enlightenment exceeds the boundary of the entire world.

═

One is greatly enlightened by taking up the three realms, by taking up one hundred grasses, by taking up the four great elements, by taking up buddha ancestors, and by taking up the fundamental point. All of these further attain great enlightenment by taking up great enlightenment. The very moment for this is just now.

═

Great enlightenment right at this moment is not self, not other.

⸻

If you speak of "achieving enlightenment," you may think that you don't usually have enlightenment. If you say, "Enlightenment comes," you may wonder where it comes from. If you say, "I have become enlightened," you may suppose that enlightenment has a beginning.

⸻

Great enlightenment is the tea and rice of daily activity.

⸻

To carry the self forward and illuminate myriad things is delusion. That myriad things come forth and illuminate the self is awakening.

Those who have great realization of delusion are buddhas; those who are greatly deluded about realization are sentient beings. Further, there are those who continue realizing beyond realization and those who are in delusion throughout delusion.

When buddhas are truly buddhas, they do not necessarily notice that they are buddhas. However, they are actualized buddhas who go on actualizing buddha.

⸻

Enlightenment is ungraspable.

⸻

Beyond enlightenment is a jewel concealed in your hair.

Circle of the Way

Dogen's teaching of the microcircle of the way is one's experience of practice-enlightenment in each moment of meditation. The macrocircle of the way is one's meditation together with all awakened ones throughout space and time. For Dogen, "Nirvana" is a nondual experience in meditation. "Intimacy" means nonseparation. As Dogen explains, continuous practice is essential for an awakened life.

On the great road of buddha ancestors there is always unsurpassable practice, continuous and sustained. It forms the circle of the way and is never cut off. Between aspiration, practice, enlightenment, and nirvana, there is not a moment's gap; continuous practice is the circle of the way. This being so, continuous practice is undivided, not forced by you or others. The power of this continuous practice confirms you as well as others. It means your practice affects the entire earth and the entire sky in the ten directions. Although not noticed by others or by yourself, it is so.

Accordingly, by the continuous practice of all buddhas and

ancestors, your practice is actualized and your great road opens up. By your continuous practice, the continuous practice of all buddhas is actualized and the great road of all buddhas opens up. Your continuous practice creates the circle of the way.

There is practice-enlightenment, which encompasses limited and unlimited life.

One time, Huineng, Old Buddha of Caoxi, asked a monk, "Do you depend upon practice and enlightenment?"

The monk replied, "It's not that there is no practice and no enlightenment. It's just that it's not possible to divide them."

This being so, know that the undividedness of practice and enlightenment is itself the buddha ancestors. It is the thunderstorm of the buddha ancestors' samadhi.

Endeavors in practice-realization of the way are not limited to one or two kinds. The thoroughly actualized realm has one thousand kinds and ten thousand ways.

The teaching of birth and death, body and mind, as the circle of the way is actualized at once. Thoroughly practicing, thoroughly clarifying, is not forced. It is just like recognizing the shadow of deluded thought and turning the light to shine within. The clarity of clarity beyond clarity prevails in the activity of buddhas. This is totally surrendering to practice.

In awakening there are aspiration, practice, enlightenment, and nirvana. Within the dream there are aspiration, practice, enlightenment, and nirvana. Every awakening within a dream is the genuine form, without regard to large or small, superior or inferior.

⸻

Intimacy renews intimacy. Because the teaching of practice-enlightenment is the way of buddha ancestors, it is intimacy that penetrates buddha ancestors. Thus intimacy penetrates intimacy.

⸻

In a circular form the blossom is full.
In transmission of the robe there is an ancient voice.
Miraculous blossoms, thousands and myriads of petals.
Fruit will naturally emerge.

⸻

Do not be concerned with who is wise and who is stupid. Do not discriminate the sharp from the dull. To practice wholeheartedly is the true endeavor of the way. Practice-realization is not defiled with specialness; it is a matter for every day.

⸻

Sitting in the meditation posture is a forthright body, a forthright mind, a forthright body-mind, a forthright buddha ancestor, a forthright practice-realization, a forthright top of the head, and a forthright life stream.

⸻

Who says the fan and the mirror are both incomplete?
This evening we all see the whole circle.
In the ocean of a billion worlds, no moment can be
measured.
The begging bowl's mouth faces the heavens.

Buddha Nature

"Buddha nature" is the capacity to become a buddha, inherent in all sentient beings according to the Mahayana teaching. Dogen interprets it as the reality of all things. A line from the Great Pari-nirvana Sutra is traditionally translated as "All living beings have buddha nature." Because of the flexible ambiguity of the Chinese language, Dogen translates it as "Living beings all are buddha nature."

Shakyamuni Buddha said, "Living beings all are buddha nature. The Tathagata is continuously abiding and not subject to change."

Thus all are buddha nature. One form of all beings is sentient beings. At this very moment, the inside and outside of sentient beings are the *all are* of buddha nature. This understanding is not only the skin, flesh, bones, and marrow of a person-to-person transmission but "You have attained my skin, flesh, bones, and marrow."

Know that the *are* of *all are buddha nature* is beyond are and are not. *All are* are the buddha words, the buddha tongue. They are the eyeball of buddha ancestors and the nostrils of patched-robed monks. The words *all are* are not limited to embryonic beings, original beings, inconceivable beings, or any other kind of beings. Furthermore, they do not mean causal beings or imaginary beings. *All are* are free from mind, object, essence, or aspects. This being so, the body, mind, and environs of *Living beings all are* [buddha nature] are not limited to the increasing power of action, imaginary causation, things as they are, or the practice-realization of miraculous powers.

⹀

Recognized or not, myriad things are just myriad things. Encountering the buddha face and the ancestor face is nothing other than fully recognizing myriad things as myriad things. Because myriad things are all-inclusive, you do not merely stand atop the highest peak or travel along the bottom of the deepest ocean. Being all-inclusive is just like this; letting go is just like that. What is called the ocean of buddha nature or Vairochana's* ocean storehouse are just myriad things. Although the ocean surface is invisible, there is no doubt about the practice of swimming in it.

⹀

Know that "when the time is ripe" means that the twelve hours of the day* are not passed in vain. "When the time is" is like saying "when the time has arrived." "When the time has arrived" is not the arrival of buddha nature. Thus, when the time has arrived, buddha nature is already actualized. This principle is self-evident. Generally, there is no time when the time has not yet arrived; there is no buddha nature that is not actualized.

⹀

A monk asked Zhaozhou, Great Master Zhenji, "Does a dog have buddha nature?"

Clarify the meaning of this question. A dog is a dog. It is not that this monk was asking whether a dog has buddha nature or not. He was asking whether an iron person still practices the way. To happen to encounter Zhaozhou's poisonous hand may look unfortunate for this monk, but it is like the lingering trace of seeing half a sage after thirty years.

Zhaozhou said, "No."

When you hear this word, a direction for study emerges. The *no* that buddha nature itself calls forth must be like this. The *no* that the dog itself calls forth must be like this. The *no* that bystanders call forth must be like this. This *no* holds the moment that dissolves a rock.

The monk said, "All sentient beings have buddha nature. How come a dog has no buddha nature?"

He meant that if sentient beings have no buddha nature, buddha nature must be *no* and a dog must be *no*. The monk asked the meaning of this. How is it that a dog's buddha nature depends upon *no?*

Zhaozhou said, "Because it has total ignorance."

He meant that *it has* is total ignorance. In the light of total ignorance and of *it has*, the dog is *no*, buddha nature is *no*. If total ignorance has not yet merged with a dog, how should a dog meet buddha nature? Even if both dog and buddha nature are let go of and taken in, still it is nothing but total ignorance all the way through.

$$\overline{}$$

As the self is activities actualized, it is not a permanent and independent self. A dog has no buddha nature; a dog has buddha nature. No beings have buddha nature; no buddha nature has beings. No buddhas have beings; no buddhas have buddhas. No buddha nature has buddha nature. No beings have beings.

─

The essential of buddha nature is that buddha nature is embodied not before but after you attain buddhahood. Buddha nature invariably arises simultaneously with attaining buddhahood. You should thoroughly investigate this principle, studying and endeavoring for twenty or thirty years. This is not something bodhisattvas of the ten stages or the three classes* can clarify.

The words "sentient beings have buddha nature" or "sentient beings have no buddha nature" point to this principle. To understand that buddha nature is embodied after attaining buddhahood is hitting a mark right on. To study otherwise is not buddha dharma. Without this understanding, buddha dharma would not have reached to this day. Not understanding this principle is not clarifying, seeing, or hearing the attainment of buddhahood.

─

Mayu,* Zen master Baoche, was fanning himself. A monk approached and said, "Master, the nature of wind is permanent and there is no place it does not reach. Why then do you fan yourself?"

"Although you understand that the nature of the wind is permanent," Mayu replied, "you do not understand the meaning of its reaching everywhere."

"What is the meaning of its reaching everywhere?" asked the monk.

Mayu just kept fanning himself.

The monk bowed deeply.

Wisdom Beyond Wisdom

The Sanskrit word prajna—*transcendental wisdom—is sometimes translated as "wisdom beyond wisdom." An essential Mahayana Buddhist teaching, it is the experience of "emptiness," or the interconnectedness of all things, and is only attained by practice. "Prajna paramita" or "actualization of prajna" is usually understood as sixfold (six paramitas): the enactment of generosity, precepts, patience, vigor, contemplation, and prajna. Dogen explains the actualization of prajna as the reality of all things classified in various ways.*

If you practice with genuine trust, you will attain the way, regardless of being sharp or dull. Do not think that buddha dharma cannot be understood in this country [Japan] because this is not a country of compassionate wisdom and people are foolish. In fact, everyone has the seed of prajna in abundance; it is only that they have rarely realized it and have not yet fully received buddha dharma.

The manifestation of the twelvefold prajna [the prajna of the six senses and their objects] means twelve types of entering [into buddha dharma].

There is the eighteenfold prajna: the prajna of eyes, ears, nose, tongue, body, and mind; the prajna of sight, sound, smell, taste, touch, and objects of mind; and the prajna of the corresponding consciousness of eyes, ears, nose, tongue, body, and mind.

There is the fourfold [noble truth] prajna: suffering, craving, freedom from suffering, and the path. There is the sixfold [manifestation] prajna: generosity, precepts, patience, vigor, contemplation, and prajna.

⸺

There is the singlefold prajna: unsurpassable, complete enlightenment, actualized at this very moment. There is the manifestation of the threefold prajna: the past, present, and future. There is the sixfold [great element] prajna: earth, water, fire, air, space, and consciousness. And there is the fourfold [bodily posture] prajna: walking, standing, sitting, and lying down, common in daily activities.

⸺

I will take refuge in this very profound manifestation of prajna. Although nothing arises or perishes in the midst of this manifestation of prajna, the precept skandha [stream], the samadhi skandha, the wisdom skandha, the emancipation skandha, and the emancipation of views skandha are established.

⸺

At the very moment of taking refuge, the prajna that establishes precepts, samadhi, wisdom, and awakening sentient beings is actualized. This prajna is called emptiness. So the actualization of emptiness is established. This is the manifestation of prajna that is extremely subtle and fathomless.

⸻

Rujing, my late master, Old Buddha, said:

> The entire body is a mouth [wind-bell] hanging in empty
>   space,
> regardless of the wind from the east, west, south, or north,
> joining the whole universe in chiming out prajna.
> *Ting-ting, ting-ting, ting-ting.*

This is an authentic heir of buddha ancestors speaking prajna. The entire body is prajna. The entire other is prajna. The entire self is prajna. The entire east, west, south, and north is prajna.

⸻

To dedicate yourself and take refuge in the manifestation of prajna is to see and uphold the Buddha, the World-Honored One. It is to be the Buddha, the World-Honored One, seeing and accepting.

Compassion

Wisdom and compassion are closely related and support each other in Buddhist teaching. Bodhisattva Avalokiteshvara is often regarded as the embodiment of compassion.

Know that when the way-seeking mind is aroused within, there is immediate freedom from fame and gain. In the vastness of the billion worlds, true heirs of dharma are rare. In spite of the long history of our country, you should make the present moment the true source, having compassion for later generations by giving emphasis to the present.

Your ability to see buddhas and hear dharma right now is the result of the compassionate continuous practice of each buddha ancestor. Without the one-to-one transmission of buddha ancestors, how could the dharma have reached us today?

If ever you value fame and gain, then be compassionate to fame and gain. If you are compassionate to fame and gain, you will not allow them to break the body that can become a buddha ancestor. Being compassionate to family and relatives is also like this. Do not think that fame and gain are phantoms and illusions but regard them as sentient beings. If you are not compassionate to fame and gain, you will accumulate unwholesome actions. The true eye of study should be like this.

Yunyan,* who would later become Great Master Wuben, asked [his senior dharma brother] Daowu,* who would later become Great Master Xiyi, "What does the bodhisattva of great compassion do with so many hands and eyes?"

Daowu said, "Like someone reaching back for the pillow at night."

Yunyan said, "I got it. I got it."

Daowu said, "What did you get?"

Yunyan said, "All over the body is hands and eyes."

Daowu said, "You have said it well. But it's eight or nine out of ten."

Yunyan said, "I am just this. How about yourself, brother?"

Daowu said, "Wherever the body reaches, it is hands and eyes."

"Giving" means nongreed. Nongreed means not to covet. Not to covet means not to curry favor. Even if you govern the Four Continents,* you should always convey the authentic path with nongreed. It is like giving away unneeded belongings to someone you don't know, offering flowers blooming on a distant mountain to the Tathagata, or again, offering treasures you had in your former life to sentient beings. Whether it is of teaching or of material, each gift has its value and is worth giving. Even if the gift is not your own, there is no reason to keep from giving. The question is not whether the gift is valuable but whether there is genuine merit.

—

Know that to give to yourself is a part of giving. To give to your family is also giving. Even when you give a particle of dust, you should rejoice in your own act because you authentically transmit the merit of all buddhas and begin to practice an act of a bodhisattva. The mind of a sentient being is difficult to change. Keep on changing the minds of sentient beings, from the moment that you offer one valuable to the moment that they attain the way. This should be initiated by giving. Thus, giving is the first of the six paramitas [manifestations].

Mind is beyond measure. Things given are beyond measure. And yet, in giving, mind transforms the gift and the gift transforms mind.

—

"Kind speech" means that when you see sentient beings, you arouse the heart of compassion and offer words of loving care. It is contrary to cruel or violent speech.

In the secular world, there is the custom of asking after someone's health. In the buddha way there is the phrase "Please treasure yourself " and the respectful address to seniors, "May I ask how you are?" It is kind speech to speak to sentient beings as you would to a baby.

Praise those with virtue; pity those without it. If kind speech is offered, little by little kind speech expands. Thus, even kind speech that is not ordinarily known or seen comes into being. Be willing to practice it for this entire present life; do not give up, world after world, life after life. Kind speech is the basis for reconciling rulers and subduing enemies. Those who hear kind speech from you have a delighted expression and a joyful mind. Those who hear of your kind speech will be deeply touched; they will always remember it.

Know that kind speech arises from kind heart, and kind heart from the seed of compassionate heart. Ponder the fact that kind speech is not just praising the merit of others; it has the power to turn the destiny of the nation.

—

Even when you are clearly correct and others are mistaken, it is harmful to argue and defeat them. On the other hand, if you admit fault when you are right, you are a coward. It is best to step back, neither trying to correct others nor conceding to mistaken views. If you don't react competitively, and let go of the conflict, others will also let go of it without harboring ill will. Above all, this is something you should keep in mind.

—

"Beneficial action" is to benefit all classes of sentient beings skillfully, that is, to care about their distant and near future and to help them by using skillful means. In ancient times, someone helped a caged tortoise; another took care of a sick sparrow. They did not expect a reward; they were moved to do so only for the sake of beneficial action.

Foolish people think that if they help others first, their own benefit will be lost, but this is not so. Beneficial action is an act of oneness, benefiting self and others together.

—

"Identity action" means nondifference. It is nondifference from self, nondifference from others. For example, in the human world the Tathagata took the form of a human being. From this we know that he did the same in other realms. When we know identity action, self and others are one.

Lute, song, and wine are one with human beings, devas, and spirit beings. Human beings are one with lute, song, and wine. Lute, song, and wine are one with lute, song, and wine. Human beings are one with human beings; devas are one with devas; spirit beings are one with spirit beings. To understand this is to understand identity action.

⸻

There are a parent and a child who are born at the same time. There are a parent and a child who die at the same time. There are a parent and a child who are born beyond time. There are a parent and a child who die beyond time.

Without hindering the compassionate parent, a child can be born. Without hindering the child, a compassionate parent is actualized.

⸻

There is a simple way to become a buddha: When you refrain from unwholesome actions, are not attached to birth and death, and are compassionate toward all sentient beings, respectful to seniors and kind to juniors, not excluding or desiring anything, with no thoughts or worries, you will be called a buddha. Seek nothing else.

⸻

"Kind mind" is parental mind. Just as parents care for their children, you should bear in mind the three treasures. Even poor or suffering people raise their children with deep love. Their hearts cannot be understood by others. This can be known only when you become a father or a mother. They do not care whether they themselves are poor or rich; their only concern is that their children will grow up. They pay no attention to whether they themselves are cold or hot but cover their children to protect them from the cold or shield them from the hot sun. This is extreme kindness. Only those who have aroused this mind can know it, and only those who practice this mind can understand it. Therefore, you should look after water and grain with compassionate care, as though tending your own children.

＝

With compassion you care for those who arrive and you nurture the monks in the community. You make the community's heart your heart and their thought of the way your thought. You make parental heart your heart and the heart of children your heart. If you practice in this way, you will be like a boat with a rudder on a wide river or like rain in a time of drought.

＝

[According to Ejo:] Dogen said, "When Eisai, the late Bishop, was abbot of the Kennin Monastery,* a man came and said, 'My family is very poor. We haven't eaten for several days. The three of us—my wife, my son, and I—are starving to death. Please show your compassion and help us.' At that time there was no clothing, food, or money in the monastery. Eisai could find no way to help. But he remembered the copper sheet intended for the halo of the Medicine Buddha* figure. He got this out, broke off a portion of it, crushed it together, and gave it to the poor man, saying, 'Please exchange this for food and satisfy your hunger.' The man departed overjoyed.

"The students were upset and said, 'That copper was for the radiance of the Medicine Buddha's image. Is it not a crime to give such sacred material to a layperson?'

"Eisai said, 'Yes, it is a crime. But think of the Buddha's intention. He gave up his own flesh and bones and offered them to sentient beings. We would honor the Buddha's intention even if we were to give the entire body of the Medicine Buddha to those who are starving now. We may fall into hell for this act. Still we should continue to save people from starvation.'

"Students nowadays should reflect on the great heart of our guiding master. Don't forget this."

Trust

Trust, also translated as faith, is one of the four pillars of Buddhism: teaching, practice, trust, and realization (kyo, gyo, shin, sho, in Japanese).

The realm of all buddhas is inconceivable. It cannot be reached by intellect—much less can those who have no trust or lack wisdom know it. Only those who have the great capacity of genuine trust can enter this realm.

≈

When genuine trust arises, practice and study with a teacher. If it does not, wait for a while. It is regrettable if you have not received the beneficence of the buddha dharma.

≈

It does not matter whether you are a layperson or a home leaver. Those who can discern excellence invariably come to trust in this practice.

≈

When the Buddha was alive, someone realized the four fruits of attainment when he was hit by a ball; another understood the great way by wearing a robe in jest. They were both ignorant people, like beasts, but with the aid of genuine trust, they were able to be free from delusion.

꠷

You attain the marrow and are invariably transmitted dharma through your utmost sincerity and trusting heart. There is no path that comes from anything other than sincere trust; there is no direction that emerges from itself.

꠷

Generally speaking, those who trust that they are within the buddha way are most rare. If you have correct trust that you are within the buddha way, you understand where the great way leads or ends and you know the original source of delusion and enlightenment. If once, in sitting, you sever the root of thinking, in eight or nine cases out of ten you will immediately attain understanding of the way.

꠷

There is a principle that views of wholesome action vary in the world. The views define what is wholesome action. It is just the same as all buddhas in the past, present, and future expounding dharma. Buddhas expounding dharma while they are in the world is just time. They expound nondiscriminating dharma according to their life span and the dimensions of their bodies.

This being so, wholesome action by a person who practices trust is far different from wholesome action by a person who practices dharma. Nevertheless, they are not two separate dharmas. It is like a shramana's keeping the precepts and a bodhisattva's breaking the precepts.

꠷

Those who have trust in dharma and practice dharma are guided in the realm of buddha ancestors and in the realm of going beyond buddha ancestors.

Know that as there are many aspects within the treasury of the true dharma eye, you cannot fully clarify it. Yet the treasury of the true dharma eye is expounded. There is no way you cannot have trust in it. Buddha sutras are like this. There are a number of them, but what you receive with trust is your one verse or your one phrase. Do not try to understand eighty thousand verses or phrases.

Know that the root of trust is not self, not others. It is not forced by the self, nor is it created by the self or led by others. Because it is not established by the self, it has been intimately entrusted throughout east and west.

The entire body embodying trust is called trust. Trust invariably follows and is followed by the stage of the buddha fruit. Without being at the stage of the buddha fruit, trust is not actualized.

Those who study the way seek to be immersed in the way. For those who are immersed in the way, all traces of enlightenment perish. Those who practice the buddha way should first of all trust in the buddha way. Those who trust in the buddha way should trust that they are in essence within the buddha way, where there is no delusion, no false thinking, no confusion, no increase or decrease, and no mistake. Arousing such trust and illuminating the way in this manner, and practicing accordingly, are fundamental in studying the way.

Women

Dogen maintained an unshakable conviction that women and men, equally, were vessels of true dharma, capable of complete realization without the slightest distinction between them. This may seem obvious in our contemporary world, but in thirteenth-century Japan, Dogen's revolutionary view challenged his students to go far beyond the constraints of culture and time.

[The Buddha's] one hundred thirty-eighth vow says, "May I attain a true awakening in the future and may women who want to leave the household in my dharma, study the way, and receive the great precepts accomplish their wishes. Until this is achieved, I will not be fully awakened."

[Question:] Should zazen be practiced by laymen and laywomen, or should it be practiced by home leavers alone?

[Dogen's answer:] The ancestors say, "In understanding buddha dharma, men and women, noble and common people are not distinguished."

Having wondrous enlightenment is an unsurpassable stage. When women become buddhas of this stage, what in all directions cannot be thoroughly experienced? Who can try to block them and keep them from arriving at this stage? They attain the power of broadly illuminating all the ten directions.

—

Those who are extremely stupid think that women are merely the objects of sexual desire and treat women in this way. The Buddha's children should not be like this. If we discriminate against women because we see them merely as objects of sexual desire, do we also discriminate against all men for the same reason?

What is the fault of women? What is the virtue of men? There are unwholesome men, and there are wholesome women. The aspiration to hear dharma and leave the household does not depend on being female or male.

—

If you vow for a long time not to look at women, do you leave out women when you vow to save numberless sentient beings? If you do so, you are not a bodhisattva. How can you call it the Buddha's compassion? This is merely nonsense spoken by a soaking-drunk shravaka. Humans and devas should not believe in such a practice.

—

Why are men special? Emptiness is emptiness. Four great elements are four great elements. Five skandhas are five skandhas. Women are just like that. Both men and women attain the way. You should honor attainment of the way. Do not discriminate between men and women. This is the most wondrous principle of the buddha way.

Before becoming free from delusion, men and woman are equally not free from delusion. At the time of becoming free from delusion and realizing the truth, there is no difference between men and women.

Zhixian [Guanxi]* of China was a revered teacher in the lineage of Linji. Once Linji saw Zhixian approaching and grabbed him.

Zhixian said, "I understand it."

Linji let him loose and said, "You are free to have a meal here."

Thus Zhixian became a student of Linji.

After leaving Linji, he went to see Moshan.*

She said, "Where are you from?"

Zhixian said, "From the entrance."

Moshan said, "Why don't you close it off?"

Zhixian was silent. He made a bow and expressed himself as a student of Moshan's. Then he asked, "How is Moshan [Mount Mo]?"

Moshan said, "It does not show its peak."

Zhixian said, "Who is the person inside the mountain?"

Moshan said, "It is beyond man and woman."

Zhixian said, "How come you don't change?"

Moshan said, "I am not a wild-fox spirit. Why should I change?"

Zhixian bowed. Then he aroused the aspiration for enlightenment and worked as head of the garden for three years.

Later he became the abbot of a monastery and said to the assembly, "I received half a ladle [of gruel] at Old Man Linji's and another half at Old Woman Moshan's. So I had a full ladle and have been satisfied up to this moment."

$$\Large =$$

[After Miaoxin* was appointed director of the guesthouse,] there was a group of seventeen monks from Shu, in the west, who were on the road in search of a master. On their way to climb up to Yangshan's* monastery, they stopped and stayed at the guesthouse. While they rested in the evening, they discussed the story about the wind and the banner of Huineng, High Ancestor of Caoxi. The seventeen monks' interpretations were all wrong.

Miaoxin, who overheard the discussion outside the room, said, "How wasteful! How many pairs of straw sandals have these seventeen blind donkeys worn out? They haven't even dreamed of buddha dharma."

Her assistant worker told them that Miaoxin had not approved their understanding. Instead of being upset with her disapproval, the monks were ashamed of their lack of understanding. They got formally dressed, offered incense, bowed, and ask her to teach.

Miaoxin said, "Come closer."

When the seventeen monks were still getting closer, Miaoxin said, "It is not that wind flaps. It is not that the banner flaps. It is not that your mind flaps."

Hearing her words, all seventeen monks had realization. They thanked her and formally became her students. Soon after, they went back to Shu without climbing up to Yangshan's monastery. Indeed, this is nothing the bodhisattvas of three classes or ten stages can come up with. It is work transmitted by buddha ancestors from heir to heir.

Deshan,* who would later become Zen Master Xuanjian, was proclaiming that he had mastered the *Diamond Sutra*,* calling himself Diamond King Chou. He claimed that he was particularly familiar with the Xinlong Commentary.* He had collected twelve bundles of commentaries. It appeared that he was incomparable. However, he was merely a descendant of dharma teachers of letters.

Once, hearing about the unsurpassable dharma transmitted heir to heir in the south, Deshan felt very competitive. He learned about the assembly of Longtan,* Zen Master Chongxin, so he crossed mountains and rivers carrying his books to meet him. On his way he stopped to catch his breath and saw an old woman.

Deshan said to her, "What do you do?"

The old woman said, "I sell rice cakes."

Deshan said, "Please sell me some."

The old woman said, "What would you do with them, reverend?"

Deshan said, "I will eat them to refresh myself."

The old woman said, "What are you carrying?"

Deshan said, "Haven't you heard of me? I am Diamond King Chou. I specialize in the *Diamond Sutra*. There is no part of it I haven't mastered. These are important commentaries on the sutra."

The old woman said, "May I ask you a question?"

Deshan said, "Of course, ask me anything."

The old woman said, "I was told that the *Diamond Sutra* says, 'The past mind is ungraspable. The present mind is ungraspable. The future mind is ungraspable.' With which mind will you satisfy your hunger with these cakes? If you can answer, I will give you some cakes. Otherwise, I will not."

Dumbfounded, Deshan was unable to answer. The old woman flapped her sleeves and went away without giving Deshan any rice cakes.

How regrettable! The king of commentators on hundreds of scrolls, a lecturer for decades, was so easily defeated by a humble old woman with a single question. There is a great difference between those who have entered an authentic teacher's chamber and received transmission and those who have not.

———

Even seven-year-old girls who practice buddha dharma and express buddha dharma are guiding teachers of the four types of disciples [monks, nuns, laymen, and laywomen]; they are compassionate parents of sentient beings. They are like dragon princesses who have attained buddhahood. You should make an offering and respect them just as you respect buddha tathagatas. This is an authentic custom of the buddha way.

Precepts

Dogen encouraged his followers to take refuge in the three trea-
sures (Buddha, Dharma, and Sangha) and receive Mahayana
precepts, also called bodhisattva precepts. They consist of the
three universal precepts and the ten prohibitory precepts.

It is taught that all buddhas in the past, present, and future leave
the household and attain the way. The twenty-eight ancestors
in India and the six early ancestors in China who transmitted
the Buddha's mind seal were all monks. They are distinguished
in the three realms by strictly observing the precepts. Thus precepts are primary for practicing Zen in pursuit of the way. How
can one become a buddha ancestor without becoming free from
faults and preventing wrongdoing?

The entire world of the ten directions is nothing but the true
human body. The coming and going of birth and death is the
true human body.

To turn this body around, abandoning the ten unwholesome
actions, keeping the eight precepts, taking refuge in the three

treasures, and leaving home and entering the homeless life, is the true study of the way. For this reason it is called the true human body. Those who follow this must not be like outsiders who hold the view of spontaneous enlightenment.

═

Ancient buddhas said:

Refrain from unwholesome action.
Do wholesome action.
Purify your own mind.
This is the teaching of all buddhas.

This teaching has been authentically transmitted from earlier buddhas to later buddhas of the future as the Seven Original Buddhas' general precepts in the ancestral school. Later buddhas received these precepts from earlier buddhas. This teaching is not limited to the Seven Original Buddhas; it is the teaching of all buddhas. Thoroughly investigate this point.

This dharma way of the Seven Original Buddhas is always the dharma way of the Seven Original Buddhas. Transmitting and receiving these precepts is a mutual activity. This is the teaching of all buddhas—the teaching, practice, and enlightenment of hundreds, thousands, and myriads of buddhas.

═

The *Guidelines for Zen Monasteries* *says:

The Mahayana *Indra's Net Sutra** expounds the ten grave and forty-eight minor precepts. Be familiar with the precepts by reading and chanting them. Know how to maintain them, how not to violate them, how to be open to them, and how to control yourself. Depend on these sacred words uttered by the [Buddha's] golden mouth and do not mistakenly follow mediocre fellows.

——

[In the ordination ceremony the officiate says:]

Good person. You have given up incorrect views and taken refuge in the true teaching. The precepts surround you.

Now take the three universal pure precepts.

[The officiate asks the recipient each of the following questions three times. The recipient affirms each question each time.]

One: The precept of observing guidelines.

Will you maintain this precept from now until you attain a buddha body?

Yes, I will maintain it.

Two: The precept of taking wholesome actions.

Will you maintain this precept from now until you attain a buddha body?

Yes, I will maintain it.

Three: The precept of benefiting all beings.

Will you maintain this precept from now until you attain a buddha body?

Yes, I will maintain it.

None of these three universal pure precepts should be violated. Will you maintain them from now until you attain a buddha body?

Yes, I will maintain them.

Please maintain them.

[The recipient makes three formal bows and kneels.]

[The officiate says:]

Good person, you have received the three universal pure precepts. Now receive the ten [prohibitory] precepts. These are the great pure precepts of all buddhas and bodhisattvas.

[The officiate asks the recipient each of the following questions three times. The recipient affirms each question each time.]

One: Not to kill.

Will you maintain this precept from now until you attain a buddha body?

Yes, I will maintain it.

Two: Not to steal.

Will you maintain this precept from now until you attain a buddha body?

Yes, I will maintain it.

Three: Not to misuse sex.

Will you maintain this precept from now until you attain a buddha body?

Yes, I will maintain it.

Four: Not to make false statements.

Will you maintain this precept from now until you attain a buddha body?

Yes, I will maintain it.

Five: Not to sell or buy alcohol.

Will you maintain this precept from now until you attain a buddha body?

Yes, I will maintain it.

Six: Not to discuss the faults of other home-leaver bodhisattvas.

Will you maintain this precept from now until you attain a buddha body?

Yes, I will maintain it.

Seven: Not to praise yourself and insult others.

Will you maintain this precept from now until you attain a buddha body?

Yes, I will maintain it.

Eight: Not to withhold dharma treasure.

Will you maintain this precept from now until you attain a buddha body?

Yes, I will maintain it.

Nine: Not to be angry.

Will you maintain this precept from now until you attain a buddha body?

Yes, I will maintain it.

Ten: Not to slander the three treasures.

Will you maintain this precept from now until you attain a buddha body?

Yes, I will maintain it.

None of these ten precepts should be violated. Will you maintain them from now until you attain a buddha body?

Yes, I will maintain them.

Please maintain them.

[The recipient makes three formal bows.]

[The officiate makes three formal bows.]

⸻

Loving fame is worse than breaking a precept. Breaking a precept is a transgression at a particular time. Loving fame is like an ailment of a lifetime. Do not foolishly hold on to fame, or do not ignorantly accept it. Not to accept fame is continuous practice. To abandon it is continuous practice.

⸻

How august!
Studying the original words

of the Seven Buddhas,
you pass beyond
the six realms.

PHILOSOPHICAL VIEW

Time

Time is experienced in a paradoxical way in meditation. Dogen's investigation of time was unique in ancient times. It is also useful for everyday life in the contemporary world. For Dogen, time is inseparable from self, from existence, and from space. Time is being. Time is no other than "time being."

You may suppose that time is only passing away and not understand that time never arrives. Although understanding itself is time, understanding does not depend on its own arrival.

People only see time's coming and going and do not thoroughly understand that the time being abides in each moment. Then, when can they penetrate the barrier? Even if people recognized the time being in each moment, who could give expression to this recognition? Even if they could give expression to this recognition for a long time, who could stop looking for the realization of the original face? According to an ordinary person's view of the time being, even enlightenment and nirvana as the time being would be merely aspects of coming and going.

Do not think that time merely flies away. Do not see flying away as the only function of time. If time merely flies away, you would be separated from time. The reason you do not clearly understand the time being is that you think of time only as passing.

━━

At the time the mountains were climbed and the rivers crossed, you were present. Time is not separate from you, and as you are present, time does not go away.

━━

In essence, all things in the entire world are linked with one another as moments. Because all moments are the time being, they are your time being.

━━

Mountains are time. Oceans are time. If they were not time, there would be no mountains or oceans. Do not think that mountains and oceans here and now are not time. If time is annihilated, mountains and oceans are annihilated. As time is not annihilated, mountains and oceans are not annihilated.

━━

The way the self arrays itself is the form of the entire world. See each thing in this entire world as a moment of time.

━━

The time being has a characteristic of flowing. So-called today flows into tomorrow, today flows into yesterday, yesterday flows into today. And today flows into today, tomorrow flows into tomorrow.

Because flowing is a characteristic of time, moments of past and present do not overlap or line up side by side. [Zen master] Qingyuan is time, Huangbo is time, Mazu is time, Shitou* is time, because self and other are already time. Practice-enlightenment is time. Being splattered with mud and getting wet with water [to awaken others] is also time.

⸺

Spring always flows through spring. Although flowing itself is not spring, flowing occurs throughout spring. Thus flowing is complete at just this moment of spring. Examine this thoroughly, coming and going.

⸺

An ancient buddha [Yaoshan*] said:

For the time being stand on top of the highest peak.
For the time being proceed along the bottom of the deepest ocean.
For the time being three heads and eight arms [of a fighting demon].
For the time being an eight- or sixteen-foot body [of the Buddha].
For the time being a staff or whisk.
For the time being a pillar or lantern.
For the time being the children of [common families] Zhang and Li.
For the time being the earth and sky.

For the time being here means time itself is being, and all being is time. A golden sixteen-foot body is time; because it is time, there is the radiant illumination of time. Study it as the twelve hours of the present. *Three heads and eight arms* is time; because it is time, it is not separate from the twelve hours of the present.

⸺

A billion worlds can be sat through within a single sitting.

⸻

The zazen of even one person at one moment imperceptibly accords with all things and fully resonates through all time. Thus, in the past, future, and present of the limitless universe, this zazen carries on the buddha's transformation endlessly and timelessly. Each moment of zazen is equally the wholeness of practice, equally the wholeness of realization.

⸻

At the very moment of embodying the awesome presence of this practice in body-mind, the timeless original practice is fully accomplished. Thus, the body-mind of this practice is originally actualized.

⸻

[According to Senne, Dogen said on a winter solstice:] Heaven has a singular clarity. Earth has renewed peacefulness. Each person attains ease. The season moves into light. This is the time when days become longer.

This is the timeless moment to attain buddha ancestors' infinite life. All of you aspire and practice within this timelessness. Endeavoring to follow the way, you must actualize one phrase. When timelessness is realized, you are powerful. When timelessness is realized, you are alive.

Bring forth the three hundred sixty days with beads made of buddha ancestor body. What do you achieve day by day? The buddha ancestor body and mind. What do you achieve day by day?

[After a pause Dogen said:] The buddha ancestors' body and mind are timelessness. Your true face is a great jewel forming in heaven. How long have you awaited timelessness? This auspicious day knows the increasing light of opportunity.

Space

For Dogen, "space" means the all-inclusive empty space that has neither boundary nor limitation. All phenomena are embraced in one moment of meditation, going beyond any distinction between small and large, near and far.

A moment or two of mind is a moment of mountains, rivers, and earth, or two moments of mountains, rivers, and earth. Because mountains, rivers, earth, and so forth neither exist nor do not exist, they are not large or small, not attainable or unattainable, not knowable or unknowable, not penetrable or impenetrable. They neither change with realization nor change without realization. Just wholeheartedly accept with trust that to study the way with mind is this mountains-rivers-and-earth mind itself thoroughly engaged in studying the way.

That which allows one part of buddha's awesome presence is the entire universe, the entire earth, as well as the entirety of birth and death, coming and going, of innumerable lands and lotus blossoms.

═

Understanding these words [about the entire universe] is going beyond buddhas and ancestors by seeing that extremely large is small and extremely small is large. Although this seems like denying that there is any such thing as large or small, this [understanding] is the awesome presence of active buddhas.

Understand that the awesome presence of the entire universe and the awesome presence of the entire earth as revealed by buddhas and ancestors is the unhidden inclusive world. This is not only the unhidden inclusive world but the awesome presence within a single active buddha.

═

Hold up empty space to build a stupa and create a buddha image. Scoop up valley water to build a stupa and create a buddha image. This is arousing the aspiration for unsurpassable, complete enlightenment. This is arousing for enlightenment one aspiration one hundred times, one thousand times, myriad times. This is practice and realization.

═

What expounds sutras is empty space [boundlessness]. Without being empty space, no one can expound even one single sutra. Expounding the *Heart Sutra* and expounding the body sutra are both done with empty space. With empty space, thinking is actualized and beyond thinking is actualized. Empty space is wisdom with a teacher, wisdom without a teacher, knowing by birth, knowing by learning. Becoming a buddha, becoming an ancestor, is also empty.

━

[Faxing Fatai* said:] "When one person opens up reality and returns to the source, the space throughout the ten directions opens up reality and returns to the source."

Realization is reality right now. Even shocks, doubts, fears, and frights are none other than reality right now. However, with buddha knowledge it is different; seeing a speck of dust is different from sitting within a speck of dust. Even when you sit in the world of phenomena, it is not broad. Even when you sit in a speck of dust, it is not narrow. If you are not fully present, you do not fully sit. If you are fully present, you are free of how broad or narrow it is where you are. Thus you have thoroughly experienced the essential unfolding of dharma blossoms.

There are those who, attracted by grass, flowers, mountains, and waters, flow into the buddha way; and there are those who, grasping soil, rocks, sand, and pebbles, uphold the buddha's seal. Although the boundless words of the Buddha permeate myriad things, the turning of the great dharma wheel is contained inside a single particle of dust.

This Saha World* can be called Shakyamuni Buddha's land. Take up this Saha World, clarify whether it is eight ounces or half a pound, and examine whether the buddha land of the ten directions is seven or eight feet.

Even if you have a good finger to grasp space, you should penetrate the inside and outside of space. You should kill space and give life to space. You should know the weight of space. You should trust that the buddha ancestors' endeavor of the way in aspiration, practice, and enlightenment through challenging dialogues is no other than grasping space.

Know that if you authentically inherit one phrase, you authentically inherit one dharma. If you inherit one phrase, you inherit mountains and you inherit waters. You cannot be separated from this very place.

Fundamental Point

The Chinese word gong'an *and its Japanese transliteration* koan *usually indicate an exemplary ancient Zen story that points students to realization. But Dogen uses this word to mean an essential experience of complete nonseparation. We translate it as "fundamental point."*

When you find your place where you are, practice occurs, actualizing the fundamental point. When you find your way at this moment, practice occurs, actualizing the fundamental point; for the place, the way, is neither large nor small, neither yours nor others'. The place, the way, has not carried over from the past, and it is not merely arising now. Accordingly, in the practice-enlightenment of the buddha way, to attain one thing is to penetrate one thing; to meet one practice is to sustain one practice.

The fundamental point actualized now is great practice.

Only buddha ancestors together with buddha ancestors have been actualizing and penetrating "the mind itself is buddha."

99

Thus it has been heard, practiced, and realized. Buddha's one hundred grasses have been taken up; they have been made to disappear. However, this cannot be explained as the sixteen-foot golden body. This is the fundamental point, which does not wait for actualization.

⸺

When the self understands, hears, and speaks the true self, invariably the fundamental point is actualized.

⸺

The self means nostrils before the birth of your parents. The nostrils, being by accident in the hand of the self, are called the entire world of the ten directions. Yet the self is right here, actualizing the fundamental point, opening the hall, and seeing the Buddha.

⸺

Speaking dharma by means of speaking dharma actualizes the fundamental point that buddha ancestors entrust to buddha ancestors. This speaking dharma is spoken by dharma.

⸺

Where water abides is not concerned with the past, future, present, or the worlds of phenomena. Yet water is the fundamental point actualized. Where buddha ancestors reach, water never fails to reach. Where water reaches, buddha ancestors never fail to be present.

⸺

Paramita means "arriving at the other shore" [of enlightenment]. Although the other shore does not have the appearance or trace from olden times, arriving is actualized. Arriving is the fundamental point. Do not think that practice leads to the other shore. Because there is practice on the other shore, when you practice, the other shore arrives. It is because this practice embodies the capacity to actualize all realms.

———

All things leave and all things arrive right here. This being so, one plants twining vines and gets entangled in twining vines. This is the characteristic of unsurpassable enlightenment. Just as enlightenment is limitless, sentient beings are limitless and unsurpassable. Just as cages and snares are limitless, emancipation from them is limitless. The actualization of the fundamental point is: "I grant you thirty blows." This is the actualization of expressing the dream within a dream.

———

The zazen I speak of is not learning meditation. It is simply the dharma gate of enjoyment and ease. It is the practice-realization of complete enlightenment. Realize the fundamental point free from the binding of nets and baskets [intellect and delusions]. Once you experience it, you are like a dragon swimming in the water or a tiger reposing in the mountains. Know that the true dharma emerges of itself, clearing away hindrances and distractions.

Duality and Nonduality

In meditation, all things can be experienced as one and not separable, which is the experience of nonduality. This is the source of compassion. At the same time, we discern things as separate with differences and boundaries. Dogen calls for the full experience of duality, of nonduality, and of freedom from duality and nonduality while maintaining integrity.

Snow

All my life, false and real, right and wrong entangled.
Playing with the moon, ridiculing wind, listening to birds,
many years were wasted seeing the mountain covered with
    snow.
This winter, I suddenly realize snow makes a mountain.

Know that water is life and air is life. The bird is life and the fish is life. Life must be the bird and life must be the fish.

When you see forms or hear sounds, fully engaging body and mind, you intuit dharma intimately. Unlike things and their reflections in the mirror, and unlike the moon and its reflection in the water, when one side is illumined, the other side is dark.

$$\Rightarrow$$

From ancient times wise people and sages have often lived on water. When they live on water they catch fish, catch human beings, and catch the way. These are all ancient ways of being on water, following wind and streams. Furthermore, there is catching the self, catching catching, being caught by catching, and being caught by the way.

$$\Rightarrow$$

There are mountains hidden in treasures. There are mountains hidden in swamps. There are mountains hidden in the sky. There are mountains hidden in mountains. There are mountains hidden in hiddenness. This is how we study.

An ancient buddha said, "Mountains are mountains, waters are waters." These words do not mean mountains are mountains; they mean mountains are mountains.

$$\Rightarrow$$

The Point of Zazen

The hub of buddhas' activity,
the turning of the ancestors' hub,
moves along with beyond thinking
and is completed in the realm of beyond merging.

As it moves along with beyond thinking
its appearing is immediate.
As it is completed in the realm of beyond merging
completeness itself is realization.

When its appearing is intimate
you have no illusion.
When completeness reveals itself
it is neither real nor apparent.

When you have immediacy without illusion
immediacy is "dropping away" with no obstacles.
Realization, beyond real or apparent,
is effort without expectation.

Clear water all the way to the bottom;
a fish swims like a fish.
Vast sky transparent throughout;
a bird flies like a bird.

There is no self—no place to hide in the all-inclusive world. There is no other—just one straight rod of iron for myriad miles. Even as branches grow thus, there is only one vehicle of dharma in the entire world. Even as leaves fall thus, things abide in their conditions and there is the aspect of the world as permanent.

Mind is all things, all things are mind. Since mind is the moon, the moon is the moon. Since mind, which is all things, is completely the moon, the all-inclusive world is the all-inclusive moon; the entire body is the entire moon. Amid the "three three before and three three after" in the myriad years of this moment, what is not the moon?

Seeing with the entire eyeball is all-inclusive study. Getting all the way through is all-inclusive study. To understand whether the face skin is thick or not is all-inclusive study.

≈

As all things are buddha dharma, there are delusion, realization, practice, birth [life] and death, buddhas and sentient beings. As myriad things are without an abiding self, there is no delusion, no realization, no buddha, no sentient being, no birth and death. The buddha way, in essence, is leaping clear of abundance and lack; thus there are birth and death, delusion and realization, sentient beings and buddhas. Yet in attachment blossoms fall, and in aversion weeds spread.

≈

When you paint spring, do not paint willows, plums, peaches, or apricots—just paint spring. To paint willows, plums, peaches, or apricots is to paint willows, plums, peaches, or apricots. It is not yet painting spring.

Body and Mind

Body and mind are not separate in buddha dharma. This being so, they are also called body-mind.

With the body and mind that migrate through birth and death, you should arouse the aspiration for enlightenment to awaken others first. Even if you spare your body and mind from the way of arousing the aspiration for enlightenment in the course of birth, aging, sickness, and death, you cannot in the end keep them as your own possessions.

Do you attain the way with the mind or the body?

Those in the house of the scriptural schools say, "You attain the way with the body, because body and mind are one." But they are not clear about how the body directly attains the way.

Now, in our house [of Zen practice], body and mind together attain the way. As long as you try to figure out buddha dharma with mind, you can never attain it even for myriad eons or thousands of lifetimes. It is attained by letting go of the mind and abandoning views and interpretations. To see form and clarify the mind, to hear sound and come to realization, is attainment of the way with the body.

Thus, when you practice just sitting and continuously give up all thoughts and views, the way becomes more and more intimate. So attaining the way means attaining it completely with the whole body. With this awareness you should sit wholeheartedly.

—

Thusness is the body and mind right now. Arouse the aspiration with this body and mind. Do not avoid stepping on water and stepping on stones. To take up just one blade of grass and create a sixteen-foot golden body, or to take up a particle of dust and build a stupa shrine of an ancient buddha, is arousing of the aspiration for enlightenment. It is to see buddha and hear buddha. It is to see dharma and hear dharma. It is to become buddha and practice buddha.

—

Since buddha ancestors are body and mind as one, one phrase or two are the buddha ancestors' warm body-mind. Their body-mind comes forth and realizes your body-mind. At the very moment of realization, this realization comes forth and realizes your body-mind. This life realizes the life of many lifetimes. By becoming a buddha and becoming an ancestor, you go beyond buddha and go beyond ancestor.

—

For the time being let us say there are two approaches to studying the buddha way: to study with mind and to study with body.

To study the way with the body means to study the way with your own body. It is the study of the way using this lump of red flesh. The body comes forth from the study of the way.

Everything that comes forth from the study of the way is the true human body.

To study with mind means to study with various aspects of mind, such as consciousness, emotion, and intellect. After resonating with the way and arousing the aspiration for enlightenment, take refuge in the great way of buddha ancestors and devote yourself to the practice of way-seeking mind. Even if you have not yet aroused the way-seeking mind, follow the examples of buddha ancestors who did arouse the way-seeking mind in former times.

—

Moment by moment a thought appears and disappears without abiding. Moment by moment a body appears and disappears without abiding. Yet the power of practice always matures.

—

Cleansing body and mind, spreading scented oil on the body after removing dirt, is a primary buddha dharma. To wear fresh clothes is a dharma of purification. By washing away dirt and spreading scented oil on the body, you become clean inside and outside. When you are clean inside and outside, your body, mind, and environs are all clean.

—

In zazen you invariably drop away body and mind, cut through fragmented concepts and thoughts from the past, and realize essential buddha dharma. You cultivate buddha activity at innumerable practice places of buddha tathagatas everywhere, provide the opportunity for everyone to engage in ongoing buddhahood, and vigorously uplift the dharma of going beyond buddha.

—

At the very moment of sitting, what is sitting? Is it an acrobat's graceful somersault or the rapid darting of a fish? Is it thinking or not thinking? Is it doing or not doing? Is it sitting within sitting? Is it sitting within body-mind? Is it sitting letting go of sitting within sitting, or letting go of sitting within body-mind? Investigate this in every possible way. Sit in the body's meditation posture. Sit in the mind's meditation posture. Sit in the meditation posture of letting go of body-mind.

All-Inclusive Mind

According to Buddhist teaching, mind is inseparable from all things or all phenomena. Subject is inseparable from object. Thus, mind is all-inclusive.

Huineng, who would later become the Thirty-third (Sixth Chinese) Ancestor, Zen Master Dajian, was staying at the Faxing Monastery,* in Guang Province, before his head was shaved.

There were two monks from India debating. One of them said, "The banner is flapping."

The other said, "The wind is flapping."

They went back and forth and could not settle the question.

Then Huineng said, "It is not the banner that is flapping. It is not the wind that is flapping. It is your mind that is flapping."

Hearing this, the monks immediately agreed with him.

Great Master Shakyamuni said [in the *Avatamsaka Sutra**], "The three realms are inseparable from single mind. There is nothing outside of mind. Mind, the Buddha, and sentient beings are not divided."

———

Mind is skin, flesh, bones, and marrow. Mind is taking up a flower and smiling. There is having mind and having no mind. There is mind with a body and mind with no body. . . . Blue, yellow, red, and white are mind. Long, short, square, and round are mind. The coming and going of birth and death are mind. Year, month, day, and hour are mind. Dream, phantom, and empty flower are mind. Water, foam, splash, and flame are mind. Spring flowers and autumn moon are mind. All things that arise and fall are mind.

———

The practice of beginner's mind is itself the entire original realization.

———

Mountains, rivers, and earth mind are just mountains, rivers, and the earth. There are no extra waves or sprays [in this mind]. The sun, the moon, and the stars mind is just the sun, the moon, and the stars. There is no extra fog or mist. The coming and going of birth and death mind is just the coming and going of birth and death. There is no extra delusion or enlightenment. The walls, tiles, and pebbles mind is just the walls, tiles, and pebbles. There is no extra mud or water. Four great elements and five skandhas mind are just four great elements and five skandhas. There is no extra horse or monkey. The chair and whisk mind is just the chair and whisk. There is no extra bamboo or wood.

———

Everyday mind is the way. "Everyday mind" means to maintain everyday mind in this world or in any world. Yesterday goes forth from this moment, and today comes forth from this place.

While going, the boundless sky goes, and while coming, the entire earth comes. This is everyday mind.

⸻

When studying in the assembly of Mazu, Fachang asked him, "What is buddha?"

Mazu said, "The mind itself is buddha."

Upon hearing these words, Fachang had realization.

Even if you arouse the aspiration for enlightenment and actualize practice-realization for a moment, that is *The mind itself is buddha*. Even if you arouse the aspiration for enlightenment and actualize practice-realization within the most minute particle, that is *The mind itself is buddha*. Even if you arouse the aspiration for enlightenment and actualize practice-realization for innumerable kalpas, that is *The mind itself is buddha*. Even if you arouse the aspiration for enlightenment and actualize practice-realization in a flash of thought, that is *The mind itself is buddha*. Even if you arouse the aspiration for enlightenment and actualize practice-realization within half a fist, that is *The mind itself is buddha*.

⸻

On Nondependence of Mind

Waterbirds
come and go,
their traces disappear—
yet they never
forget their path.

Life and Death

Life is often called "birth" in Buddhism, since a person is seen as being born and dying many times at each moment. Thus birth and death are experienced not in opposition but as one. To indicate this unity, we sometimes translate them as birth-and-death. In meditation one may experience a state beyond birth and beyond death.

———————————

The great way of all buddhas, thoroughly practiced, is emancipation and realization.

"Emancipation" means that in birth you are emancipated from birth and in death you are emancipated from death. Thus there is detachment from birth-and-death and penetration of birth-and-death. Such is the complete practice of the great way. There is letting go of birth-and-death and vitalizing birth-and-death. Such is the thorough practice of the great way.

"Realization" is birth; birth is realization. At the time of realization there is nothing but birth totally actualized, nothing but death totally actualized.

Such activity makes birth wholly birth and death wholly

death. Actualized just so at this moment, this activity is neither large nor small, neither immeasurable nor measurable, neither remote nor near. Birth right now is undivided activity. Undivided activity is birth right now.

You should understand that birth-and-death is itself nirvana. Nirvana is not realized outside of birth-and-death.

Know that birth-and-death is the activity of the buddha way; birth-and-death is the furnishings [essentials] of the buddha house. It is utilized when it needs to be utilized; it is fully clarified when it is clarified. Accordingly, all buddhas are clear about the implements of birth-and-death and fully achieve their utilization.

Shenshan,* who would later become Zen Master Sengmi, was traveling with Dongshan,* who would later become Zen Master Wuben.

Dongshan pointed to a temple near the road and said, "Inside that temple someone is speaking of mind, speaking of essence."

Shenshan said, "Who is that?"

Dongshan said, "My dharma uncle, your question has completely killed that person."

Shenshan said, "Who is speaking of mind, speaking of essence?"

Dongshan said, "In death, find life."

Birth is just like riding in a boat. You raise the sails and you steer. Although you maneuver the sail and the pole, the boat gives you a ride, and without the boat you couldn't ride. But you ride in the boat, and your riding makes the boat what it is. Investigate a moment such as this. At just such a moment, there is nothing but the world of the boat. The sky, the water, and the shore are all the boat's world, which is not the same as a world that is not the boat's. Thus you make birth what it is; you make birth your birth.

When you ride in a boat, your body, mind, and environs together are the undivided activity of the boat. The entire earth and the entire sky are both the undivided activity of the boat. Thus birth is nothing but you; you are nothing but birth.

The Buddha said, "This man is not as fast as a demon who runs on the ground. This demon is not as fast as a flying demon. This flying demon is not as fast as the four deva kings. These deva kings are not as fast as the sun and the moon. The sun and the moon are not as fast as the devas who pull the cart of the sun and the moon. These devas fly around very fast. However, the change of life through birth and death is faster than these devas. It flows moment by moment without stopping."

How our life changes moment by moment, flowing through birth and death, is like this. You practitioners should not forget it for even an instant of thought. If you arouse the thought of bringing others across first while in this swift change through birth and death, a timeless lifespan is immediately actualized.

In regard to freely penetrating the great way that completes birth and masters death, there is an ancient statement, "A great sage surrenders birth and death to the mind, surrenders birth and death to the body, surrenders birth and death to the way, surrenders birth and death to birth and death." As this teaching is actualized without limitation in the past and present, the awesome presence of active buddhas is thoroughly practiced immediately.

⸻

Within the cycles of birth and death for myriad kalpas, one day of continuous practice is a bright jewel in the banded hair, the ancient mirror of all-inclusive birth and all-inclusive death. It is a day of rejoicing. The power of continuous practice is itself rejoicing.

⸻

Although there is birth and death in each moment of this life of birth and death, the body after the final body is never known. Even though you do not know it, if you arouse the aspiration for enlightenment, you will move forward on the way of enlightenment. The moment is already here. Do not doubt it in the least. Even if you should doubt it, this is nothing but everyday mind.

⸻

In birth there is nothing but birth, and in death there is nothing but death. Accordingly, when birth comes, face and actualize birth, and when death comes, face and actualize death. Do not avoid them or desire them.

⸻

Firewood becomes ash, and it does not become firewood again. Yet do not suppose that the ash is after and the firewood before. Understand that firewood abides in its condition as firewood, which fully includes before and after, while it is independent of before and after. Ash abides in its condition as ash, which fully includes before and after. Just as firewood does not become firewood again after it is ash, you do not return to birth after death.

This being so, it is an established way in buddha dharma to

deny that birth turns into death. Accordingly, birth is understood as beyond birth. It is an unshakable teaching in the Buddha's discourse that death does not turn into birth. Accordingly, death is understood as beyond death.

Birth is a condition complete this moment. Death is a condition complete this moment. They are like winter and spring. You do not call winter the beginning of spring nor summer the end of spring.

⸻

Given to Hironaga Hatano *

The whole universe
shatters into a hundred pieces.
In the great death
there is no heaven, no earth.
Once body and mind have turned over,
there is only this to say:
past mind cannot be grasped,
present mind cannot be grasped,
future mind cannot be grasped.

Karma

Karma is a Sanskrit word meaning an action and its visible and invisible effect. Dogen had a deep belief that any action can become a cause that brings forth an effect sooner or later.

———————————

The real issue here, to clarify birth and to clarify death, is the great matter of causes and effects in the buddha house.

≈

Cause is not before and effect is not after. Cause is complete and effect is complete. Cause is all-inclusive, just as dharma is all-inclusive. Effect is all-inclusive, just as dharma is all-inclusive. Although effect is experienced, induced by cause, one is not before and the other is not after. We say that both before and after are all-inclusive.

≈

From the present existence you reach an intermediary existence, and from an intermediary existence you reach a future existence, passing through moment by moment. In this way, beyond your intention, you pass through birth and death driven by your karma, without stopping even for a moment

≈

The World-Honored One said, "Effects of an action will never perish, even after one hundred and one thousand eons. One receives the results when the causes and conditions meet. Know that dark actions bring forth dark results, bright actions bring forth bright results, and mixed actions bring forth varied results. So refrain from taking dark and mixed actions and endeavor to take bright actions."

———

There are no exceptions. Those who act in an unwholesome way decline, and those who act in a wholesome way thrive. There is not a hairbreadth of discrepancy. If cause and effect had been ignored or denied, buddhas would not have appeared and Bodhidharma would not have come from India; sentient beings would not have seen Buddha or heard the dharma.

———

Baizhang,* Zen Master Dahui of Mount Baizhang, Hao Region, was the dharma heir of Mazu. His priest name is Huaihai. When Baizhang gave teachings to the assembly, an old man would often appear and listen to his dharma talks. The old man usually left after the talks, but one day he remained behind.

Baizhang asked, "Who are you?" The old man said, "I am not actually a human being. In ancient times, at the time of Kashyapa Buddha, I lived and taught on this mountain. One day a student asked, 'Does a person who has cultivated great practice still fall into cause and effect?' I said to him, 'No, such a person does not fall into cause and effect.' Because of this I was reborn as a wild fox for five hundred lifetimes. Venerable Master, please say a turning word and free me from this body of a wild fox." Then he asked Baizhang, "Does a person who has cultivated great practice still fall into cause and effect?"

Baizhang said, "Do not ignore cause and effect."

Immediately the old man had great realization.

⸺

The most serious mistake made by those who study Zen in China is to believe that a person who practices completely does not fall into cause and effect.

⸺

Immediately clarify all causes and all effects if you want to make the aspiration for enlightenment your priority, and so respond to the boundless gift of buddha ancestors.

⸺

Reflect quietly and rejoice that although we live in the last five hundred years [of the three periods of five hundred years after the time of Shakyamuni Buddha] in a faraway island of a remote country, as our wholesome karma from the past has not decayed, we have authentically received the awesome procedure of ancient buddhas, practice it, and realize it without staining it.

⸺

Ignoring causation invites disaster. Past sages clarified cause and effect, but students have become confused in recent times. Those of you who have a pure aspiration for enlightenment and want to study buddha dharma for the sake of buddha dharma should clarify causation as past sages did.

⸺

Venerable Kumaralabha,* the Nineteenth Ancestor, journeyed to central India, where he met a seeker called Jayata,* who asked him, "My parents follow the path of the three treasures, but they have been sick, and nothing they do goes well. Our next-door neighbors have been engaged in the low practice of slaughtering animals, yet they are healthy and content. How come they are happy while we are so unfortunate?"

Kumaralabha said, "Why should you doubt? The results from our wholesome and unwholesome actions take effect in the three periods. But people only see that the peaceful die young and the violent live long, or that the unrighteous prosper and the righteous decline. They deny the law of cause and effect and say that our sins and good deeds are without consequences. They do not know that the shadows and echoes follow our actions without a hairbreadth's gap. The results of our actions don't get worn away even in one hundred, one thousand, or ten thousand eons."

Hearing these words, Jayata was freed from his doubt.

What Kumaralabha meant by *the results from our wholesome and unwholesome actions take effect in the three periods* is:

One: the result received in this lifetime.
Two: the result received in the next lifetime.
Three: the result received in a lifetime after the next.

These are called the three periods. From the beginning of learning the way of buddha ancestors, we study and clarify the principle of the effects of karma in the three periods. If we don't, many of us will make a mistake and fall into crooked views. Not only do we fall into crooked views, we get into unwholesome realms and experience suffering for a long time. When we do not maintain wholesome roots, we lose a great deal of merit and are obstructed for a long time from the path of enlightenment. Would this not be regrettable?

Freedom

Freedom in Zen practice is not to do whatever one wants but to break through the seeming boundaries of subject and object as well as the distinctions between delusion and enlightenment that hinder us from the realization of things as they are.

[Keizan Jokin* said:] Priest Eihei Dogen, the Fifty-first Ancestor, practiced with priest Rujing of Tiantong. One day during the late evening zazen, Rujing said to the assembly, "Practicing Zen is dropping away body and mind."

Upon hearing this, Dogen suddenly had great realization. Immediately [after zazen], he went up to the abbot's quarters and offered incense to Rujing, who said, "Why are you offering incense to me?"

Dogen said, "I have dropped away body and mind."

Rujing said, "You have dropped away body and mind. Your body and mind have been dropped away."

Dogen said, "This is a temporary matter. Please don't approve me easily."

Rujing said, "I am not approving you easily."

Dogen said, "What is not approving easily?"

Rujing said, "Dropping away body and mind."

Dogen bowed deeply.

Rujing said, "Dropping away has dropped away."

At that moment the attendant monk Guanping from the Fu Region said, "This person from a foreign country has achieved what-it-is. Indeed, this is not a minor thing."

Rujing said, "How many blows of the fist have you received with this understanding? Dropping away serene composure is thunder and lightning."

⸻

The concentrated endeavor of the way I am speaking of allows all things to come forth in realization to practice going beyond in the path of letting go. Passing through the barrier [of dualism] and dropping off limitations in this way, how could you be hindered by nodes in bamboo or knots in wood [concepts and theories]?

⸻

All-inclusive study is just single-minded sitting, dropping away body and mind. At the moment of going there, you go there; at the moment of coming here, you come here. There is no gap.

⸻

In stillness, mind and object merge in realization and go beyond enlightenment.

⸻

The embodiment of buddha is not becoming a buddha. When you break through the snares and cages [of words and concepts], a sitting buddha does not hinder becoming a buddha. Right now you have the ability to enter the realm of buddha and enter the realms of demons throughout the ages. Going forward and going backward, you personally have the freedom of overflowing ditches, overflowing valleys.

⸗

"Freedom" means the undivided activity of mind that is actualized.

⸗

Enlightenment disappears in the practice of letting go. This is the everyday activity of buddha ancestors.

⸗

One day while Xiangyan was sweeping the path, a pebble flew up and struck a bamboo. At the unexpected sound, he had thorough awakening. After bathing and cleansing himself, he faced Mount Gui, offered incense, prostrated himself, and said, "Master, if you had spoken for me at that time, this could not have happened. Your kindness is deeper than my parents'." Then he wrote a poem:

> One stroke dissolves knowledge,
> struggle no longer needed.
> I will follow the ancient path,
> not lapsing into quietude.
> Noble conduct beyond sound and form—
> no trace anywhere.
> Those who have mastered the way
> may call this an unsurpassable activity.

Xiangyan presented this poem to Guishan, who said, "This fellow has gone through."

⸗

Know that when sentient beings leap beyond and attain true awakening, they are buddha ancestors; disciples and teachers of buddha ancestors; and the skin, flesh, bones, and marrow of buddha ancestors.

＝

When you leap beyond delusion and enlightenment, dharma blossoms turn dharma blossoms.

Nature

*For Dogen, every element of the natural world is inseparable
from one's mind. Mountains practice with one who meditates.
Water realizes the way with one who practices.*

Original Face

Flowers in spring,
cuckoos in summer,
moon in autumn,
snow in winter,
serene and cool.

≈

When you turn the four great elements and the five skandhas
and practice sincerely, you attain the way. When you turn grass,
trees, tiles, and walls and practice sincerely, you attain the way.
It is so because the four great elements and the five skandhas, as
well as grass, trees, tiles, and walls, practice together with you.
They have the same nature, the same mind and life, the same
body and capacity as you.

≈

Saying that the self returns to the self is not contradicted by saying that the self is mountains, rivers, and the great earth.

$$\Longrightarrow$$

All buddhas are wind and rain, water and fire.

$$\Longrightarrow$$

Because mountains are high and broad, their way of riding the clouds always extends from the mountains; their wondrous power of soaring in the wind comes freely from the mountains.

$$\Longrightarrow$$

Because earth, grass, trees, walls, tiles, and pebbles of the world of phenomena in the ten directions all engage in buddha activity, those who receive the benefits of the wind and water are inconceivably helped by the buddha's transformation, splendid and unthinkable, and intimately manifest enlightenment. Those who receive these benefits of water and fire widely engage in circulating the buddha's transformation based on original realization. Because of this, all those who live with you and speak with you also receive immeasurable buddha virtue, practice continuously, and extensively unfold the endless, unremitting, unthinkable, unnamable buddha dharma throughout the entire world of phenomena.

$$\Longrightarrow$$

Although there are many features in the dusty world and the world beyond conditions, you see and understand only what your eye of practice can reach. In order to learn the nature of the myriad things, you must know that although they may look round or square, the other features of oceans and mountains are infinite in variety; whole worlds are there. It is so not only around you but also directly beneath your feet or in a drop of water.

≡

In Song China there was a man who called himself Layman Dongpo.* He was originally named Shi of the Su family, and his initiatory name was Zidan. A literary genius, he studied the way of dragons and elephants in the ocean of awakening. He descended into deep chasms and soared freely through clouds.

One night when Dongpo visited Mount Lu, he was enlightened upon hearing the sound of the valley stream. He composed the following verse, which he presented to Changzong:*

Valley sounds are the long broad tongue.
Mountain colors are no other than the unconditioned
body.
Eighty-four thousand verses are heard through the night.
What can I say about this in the future?

Seeing this verse, Changzong approved his understanding.

≡

Are mountain colors and valley sounds one phrase or half a phrase? Are they eighty-four thousand verses of scripture? You may regret that mountains and waters conceal sounds and colors, but you may also rejoice that the moment of enlightenment emerges through mountains and waters.

≡

One spring day after practicing for thirty years, Lingyun,* who would later become Zen Master Zhiqin, walked into the mountains. While resting he saw peach blossoms in full bloom in a distant village and was suddenly awakened. He wrote this poem, which he presented to Guishan:

For thirty years I have looked for a sword master.
Many times leaves fell, new ones sprouted.
One glimpse of peach blossoms—
now no more doubts, just this.

Guishan said, "One who enters with ripened conditions will never leave." He approved Lingyun in this way.

<hr/>

Mountains and waters right now actualize the ancient buddha expression. Each, abiding in its condition, unfolds its full potential. Because mountains and waters have been active since before the Empty Eon, they are alive at this moment. Because they have been the self since before form arose, they are emancipation actualized.

<hr/>

Mountains' walking is just like human walking. Accordingly, do not doubt mountains' walking even though it does not look the same as human walking.

<hr/>

All waters appear at the foot of the eastern mountains. Accordingly, all mountains ride on clouds and walk in the sky. All mountains are the head tops of all waters. Walking beyond and walking within are both done on water. All mountains walk with their toes on waters and make them splash. Thus, in walking there are seven vertical paths and eight horizontal paths. This is practice-realization.

<hr/>

An ancient buddha said, "Mountains, rivers, and earth are born at the same moment with each person. All buddhas of the past, present, and future are practicing together with each person."

If we look at mountains, rivers, and earth when a person is born, this person's birth does not seem to be bringing forth additional mountains, rivers, and earth on top of the existing ones. Yet the ancient buddha's word should not be a mistake. How should we understand this? Even if you do not understand it, do not ignore it but be determined to understand it. Since this word is already expounded, listen to it. Listen until you understand.

———

When the time comes, flowers open. This is the moment of flowers, the arrival of flowers. At this very moment of flowers arriving, there is no other way. Plum and willow flowers unfailingly bloom on plum and willow trees. You see the flowers and know plum and willow trees. You understand flowers by looking at plum and willow trees. Peach and apricot flowers have never bloomed on plum and willow trees. Plum and willow flowers bloom on plum and willow trees. Peach and apricot flowers bloom on peach and apricot trees. Flowers in the sky bloom in the sky in just this way. They do not bloom on other grasses or trees.

———

When the old plum tree suddenly blooms, the world of blossoming flowers arises. At the moment when the world of blossoming flowers arises, spring arrives. There is a single blossom that opens five petals. At this moment of a single blossom, there are three, four, and five blossoms, hundreds, thousands, myriads, billions of blossoms—countless blossoms.

———

To follow ancient examples means to allow the eye of the ancestral school to see directly and to allow the ear beyond time to hear with humility. It is to gouge out the vast open sky and settle your body in it, to pierce through the skull of the world and just sit. You open the fist and you stay with the nostril. You dye the white cloud within the blue sky, stir up autumn water, and wash the bright moon.

＝

The coming and going of birth and death is the coming and going of radiant light. Going beyond ordinary and sacred is the blue and red of radiant light. Becoming a buddha and becoming an ancestor is the black and yellow of radiant light. It is not that there is no practice-realization; it is just defilement [expression] of radiant light. Grass, trees, tiles, and walls, as well as skin, flesh, bones, and marrow, are the red and white of radiant light. Haze, mist, water, and rocks, as well as the path of a bird and the profound way, are rotating circles of radiant light.

＝

Both blossoms and fruit maintain moments. All moments maintain blossoms and fruit. This being so, one hundred grasses all have blossoms and fruit. All trees have blossoms and fruit. Trees of gold, silver, copper, iron, coral, and crystal all have blossoms and fruit. Trees of earth, water, fire, air, space, all have blossoms and fruit. Human trees have blossoms. Decayed trees have blossoms.

＝

Know that even though the moon passes quickly, it is beyond beginning, middle, or end. Thus there is the first-month moon and the second-month moon. The first and the second are both the moon. Right practice is the moon. Right offering is the moon. Snapping the sleeves and walking away is the moon.

Round and pointed are not concerned with the cycle of coming and going. The moon is beyond coming and going; it goes freely and grasps firmly coming and going, beyond coming and going. Manifesting wind and streams, the moons are as they are.

Miracles

Traditionally, the six types of supernormal powers are regarded as miracles. They are the celestial feet, the celestial eye, the celestial ear, seeing others' minds, knowing the past, and the power to be free from desire. Dogen calls them minor miracles and encourages practitioners to experience the miracles of each moment.

The miracles I am speaking of are the daily activities of buddhas, which they do not neglect to practice. There are six miracles [freedom from the six-sense desires], one miracle, going beyond miracles, and unsurpassable miracles. Miracles are practiced three thousand times in the morning and eight hundred times in the evening.

Miracles arise simultaneously with buddhas but are not known by buddhas. Miracles disappear with buddhas but do not overwhelm buddhas.

Guishan is the Thirty-seventh Ancestor, a direct descendant of Shakyamuni Buddha. He was a dharma heir of Baizhang, Zen

Master Dazhi. Today buddha ancestors in the ten directions, even those who do not call themselves descendants of Guishan, are all in fact his remote descendants.

One day while Guishan was lying down, Yangshan Huiji came to see him. Guishan turned to face the wall.

Yangshan said, "I am your student. Please don't be formal."

Guishan started to get up.

Yangshan rose to leave.

Guishan said, "Huiji."

Yangshan returned.

Guishan said, "Let me tell you about my dream."

Yangshan leaned forward to listen.

Guishan said simply, "Would you interpret my dream for me? I want to see how you do it."

In response, Yangshan brought a basin of water and a towel. Guishan washed his face and sat up. Then Xiangyan came in.

Guishan said, "Huiji and I have been sharing miracles. This is no small matter."

Xiangyan said, "I was next door and heard you."

Guishan said to him, "Why don't you try now?"

Xiangyan made a bowl of tea and brought it to him.

Guishan praised them, saying, "You two students surpass even Shariputra* and Maudgalyayana* with your miraculous activity!"

<hr>

Encompassed by the power of great miracles, minor miracles occur. Great miracles include minor miracles, but minor miracles do not know great miracles. Minor miracles are a tuft of hair breathing in the vast ocean, a mustard seed storing Mount Sumeru, the top of the head spouting water, or feet spreading fire. Miracles like these are minor miracles. The five or six miraculous powers are minor miracles.

⸺

The teaching, practice, and enlightenment of buddhas are all actualized through miracles. They are actualized not only in the realm of buddhas but also in the realm of going beyond buddhas. The transformative power of miracle buddhas is indeed beyond thinking. This power appears before the buddha bodies appear and is not concerned with the past, present, or future. The aspiration, practice, enlightenment, and nirvana of all buddhas would not have appeared without buddha miracles.

⸺

Layman Pangyun* was an outstanding person in the ancestral seat. He not only trained with Mazu and Shitou but met and studied with many other enlightened teachers. One day he said, "Miracles are nothing other than fetching water and carrying firewood."

Thoroughly investigate the meaning of these words. *Fetching water* means to draw and carry water. Sometimes you do it yourself and sometimes you have others do it. Those who practice this are all miracle buddhas. Although miracles are noticed once in a while, miracles are miracles. It is not that things perish or are eliminated when they are unnoticed. Things are just as they are even when unnoticed. Even when people do not know that fetching water is a miracle, fetching water is undeniably a miracle.

Carrying firewood means doing the labor of hauling, as in the time of Huineng, the Sixth Ancestor. Even if you do not know that miracles happen three thousand times in the morning and eight hundred times in the evening, miracles are actualized.

Those who see and hear the wondrous activities of miracles by buddha tathagatas do not fail to attain the way. Attaining the way of all buddhas is always completed by the power of miracles.

Causing water to spout out of the head is a practice of the Lesser Vehicles.* It is merely a minor miracle. On the other hand, fetching water is a great miracle. The custom of fetching water and carrying firewood has not declined, as people have not ignored it. It has come down from ancient times to today, and it has been transmitted from there to here. Thus miracles have not declined even for a moment.

The miracles transmitted by buddha ancestors are as Baizhang described. A miracle buddha is one who goes beyond buddha, a most wondrous person, an uncreated self, a bodhisattva of going beyond miracles. Miracles do not depend upon intellectual understanding, do not abide in themselves, and are not hindered by things. There are the six types of miracles in the buddha way, which have been maintained by buddhas ceaselessly. There has not been a single buddha who has not maintained them. Those who do not maintain them are not buddhas. These six types of miracles leave no trace in the six-sense organs.

The buddha dharma is always actualized through miracles. When actualized, a drop of water swallows the great ocean and a speck of dust hurls out a high mountain. Who can doubt that these are miracles?

STUDENTS AND TEACHERS

Affinity and Merging

For Dogen, the teacher and student are united through affinity with dharma and with each other. They merge in realization and become one.

─────────────────

In the practice of unsurpassable, complete enlightenment, what is most difficult is to find a guiding teacher. The guiding teacher should be a strong person, regardless of being a male or female. The teacher should be a person of thusness, with excellent knowledge and wild-fox [transformative] spirit, whether living in the past or in the present.

≈

Endeavor wholeheartedly to follow the path of earlier sages. You may have to climb mountains and cross oceans when you look for a teacher to inquire about the way. Look for a teacher and search for understanding with all-encompassing effort, as if you were coming down from heaven or emerging from the ground. When you encounter a true teacher, you invoke sentient beings as well as insentient beings. You hear with the body, you hear with the mind.

≈

In response to affinity [between buddhas and sentient beings, and also between the teacher and the student], the aspiration for enlightenment arises. It is not given by buddhas or bodhisattvas, and it is not created by you. The aspiration arises in response to affinity.

⸺

Just understand that when a master who has attained the way with a clear mind authentically transmits to a student who has merged with realization, then the wondrous dharma of the Seven Original Buddhas, in its essence, is actualized and maintained. This cannot be known by those who study words. Therefore, set aside your doubt, practice zazen under an authentic teacher, and actualize buddhas' receptive samadhi.

⸺

When Shakyamuni Buddha taught at Vulture Peak, Bhaishajyaraja Bodhisattva* said to the assembly, "If you get close to a dharma teacher, you will directly attain the bodhisattva way. If you follow the teacher and practice, you will see as many buddhas as the sands of the Ganges."

⸺

I recommend to students who are already studying with a teacher, as well as all those outstanding people who seek the truth of buddha dharma, to practice zazen and endeavor in the way under the guidance of an authentic teacher and investigate the teaching of the buddha ancestors without distinguishing between beginning or advanced and without being concerned about ordinary or sacred.

⸺

Don't scold or criticize monks with harsh words. Even when they make mistakes, don't put them down angrily. Whatever mistakes they make, if there are more than four monks assembled and practicing together, they should be respected as a treasure of the nation. Abbots, elders, and teachers should give them thorough instruction with a grandmotherly, compassionate heart. Those who need to be hit should be hit, and those who need to be scolded should be scolded, but don't insult or slander them.

When my late teacher Rujing was abbot of the Tiantong Monastery, he criticized some monks and hit them with his slipper during zazen to keep them awake. Those who were hit appreciated it and admired him.

He said in a lecture, "I am old now, overdue to be retired, passing my last years in a hut. But I'm here as abbot to help break your delusions and to assist in your practice of the way. For this reason, I sometimes scold you or hit you with a bamboo stick. But this is a dangerous thing to do. I only do this to guide you on behalf of the Buddha. My brothers, please pardon me with compassionate heart."

When he said this, all the monks wept. Guide people and extend the teaching with this heart. Even those who are in the position of abbot or elder should not scold and control the monks as if they were personal possessions.

Furthermore, it is an error to discuss others' shortcomings and make accusations in their absence. Be extremely cautious of this. When you see others' faults, use skillful means not to arouse their anger. If you talk about their fault as if it were somebody else's, it will be easier for them to accept your point.

⸻

When you penetrate the moment of Mahakashyapa transmitting to Ananda,* Ananda hides his body in Mahakashyapa, and

Mahakashyapa hides his body in Ananda. Thus, at the moment of [teacher and student] meeting for transmission, the practice of exchanging face, skin, flesh, bones, and marrow cannot be avoided.

⸺

As he was a person of thusness, Huineng attained clarity. Later he went to Mount Huangmei and met Hongren, Zen Master Daman. Hongren then assigned him to work as a laborer. Huineng pounded rice day and night for eight months.

Once, in the middle of the night, Hongren slipped into the pounding hut and asked Huineng, "Is the rice hulled now?"

Huineng said, "Hulled but not yet sifted."

Hongren tapped the mortar with his cane three times. Huineng shuffled the rice three times. This is regarded as the moment when teacher and student merged. Although neither known by the self nor understood by others, the transmission of dharma and the transmission of the robe took place at this very moment of thusness.

⸺

In Honor of Master Rujing

I use this wooden dipper to stir up wind and waves.
The profound power of his great teaching asks for an
    equal response.
Even when the plum has wilted and winter has reached its
    deepest cold,
do not let your body be numb or your mind absent.

⸺

[According to Ejo, at one ceremony for Shakyamuni Buddha's enlightenment, held on the eighth day of the twelfth month, Dogen said:]

At night amid the withered grass, after practicing for six
    years,
a monk thoughtlessly drifts among the plum blossoms.

A spring wind rises. Red and white branches are proud of themselves. Senior monks, do you want to know the cause of Monk Gautama's enlightenment? One: hearing Tiantong's words of dropping off, I attained the buddha way. Two: using my fist, I, Daibutsu, enter your eyeballs. With miraculous wisdom the buddha transforms sentient beings. Seeing the morning star, all of a sudden he steals your entire body while sitting on the diamond seat.

Grasping and letting go is clearly one activity, encountering thirty-three generations of Indian and Chinese ancestors all at once. So how is the World-Honored One's life-root in your own hands? Do you still want to meet the World-Honored One?

[Dogen raised his fist for a while, then spread his five fingers and continued to speak:] You all have just met the World-Honored One. After having met him, how is it?

[Dogen paused again, and then went on:] At the very moment of attaining enlightenment upon seeing the morning star, this is where the Tathagata eats his morning gruel.

Lay Practice

The Buddhist community consists of four types of practitioners: monks, nuns, laymen, and laywomen. Dogen's statement on lay practitioners changes from the time he wrote "Recommending Zazen to All People" in his early teaching career to the later period when he dedicated his life to training monastic practitioners.

When the Buddha was at the Banyan Grove in Kapilavastu,* Mahanaman of the Shakya Clan* came to him and said, "What is a layperson?"

The Buddha said, "If a good man or a good woman whose senses are open takes refuge in the three treasures, the person is called a layperson."

Mahanaman said, "What is a partial layperson?"

The Buddha said, "Mahanaman, one who takes refuge in the three treasures and receives even one precept [receiving the five precepts in stages], that person is called a partial layperson.

Question: Should zazen be practiced by laymen and laywomen, or should it be practiced by home leavers alone?

Answer: The ancestors say, "In understanding buddha dharma, men and women, noble and common people, are not distinguished."

⸺

Lay bodhisattvas also wear kashayas. In China, Emperor Wu of the Liang Dynasty* and Emperor Yang of the Sui Dynasty* both wore a kashaya. Emperors Dai and Su* [of the Tang Dynasty] also wore a kashaya, studied with monks, and received the bodhisattva precepts. Other laymen and laywomen of the past and present have also received a kashaya together with the Buddhist precepts.

⸺

I rejoice that the vow I made at that time [when I first saw monks putting on the kashaya at Tiantong] has not been in vain and that there have been many bodhisattvas, lay and ordained, who have received the kashaya in Japan. Those who maintain the kashaya should always venerate it day and night. This brings forth most excellent merit.

⸺

Those who are called laity in Song China are people who have not left their households. Some of them are married and have their abodes. Others are celibate but may still have much worldly concern. However, monks with cloud robes and mist sleeves visit laypeople who have clarified dharma, bow to them, and inquire about the way, just as they do to masters who have left their households. They should also do so to accomplished women and even to animals.

⸺

Buddha ancestors, out of their kindness, have opened the wide gate of compassion in order to let all sentient beings enter realization. Who among humans and heavenly beings cannot enter?

If you look back to ancient times, the examples are many. To begin with, Emperors Dai and Shun had many obligations on the throne; nevertheless, they practiced zazen in pursuit of the way and penetrated the great way of buddha ancestors. Ministers Li and Fang* both closely served their emperors, but they practiced zazen, pursued the way, and entered realization in the great way of buddha ancestors.

This just depends on whether you have the willingness or not. It does not matter whether you are a layperson or a home leaver. Those who can discern excellence invariably come to trust in this practice. Those who regard worldly affairs as a hindrance to buddha dharma think only that there is no buddha dharma in the secular world; they do not understand that there is no secular world in buddha dharma.

Recently, there was a high official of Great Song, Minister Feng,* who was an adept in the ancestral way. He once wrote a poem concerning his view of practice:

I enjoy zazen between my official duties
and seldom sleep lying on a bed.
Although I appear to be a minister,
I'm known as a Buddhist elder throughout the country.

Although he was busy in his official duties, he attained the way because he had a deep intention toward the buddha way. When considering someone like him, reflect on yourself and illuminate the present with the past.

In Song China, kings and ministers, officials and common people, men and women, grounded their intention on the ancestral way. Both warriors and literary people aroused the intention to practice Zen and study the way. Among those who pursued this intention, many of them illuminated their mind-ground. From this we understand that worldly duties do not hinder the buddha dharma.

When the true buddha dharma is spread widely in the nation, the rule of the monarch is peaceful because all buddhas and devas protect it unceasingly. If the rule is peaceful, the buddha dharma gains eminence.

When Shakyamuni Buddha was alive, even those who previously had committed serious crimes or had mistaken views attained the way. In the assemblies of the ancestors, hunters and woodcutters attained enlightenment. As it was so for them at that time, it is so for anyone now. Just seek the teaching of an authentic master.

—

Those who have not left the household do not succeed in the right action of buddha ancestors, nor do they authentically transmit the great way of buddha dharma. Although laypeople study the way as laymen and laywomen, there is no precedent of their mastering the way. At the time of mastering the way, people invariably leave the household. How can those who cannot bear to leave the household succeed in the rank of buddhas?

A layperson may have a fair share of merit for having a wholesome root but may ignore acquiring the merit of having the wholesome root of body-mind. This being so, during the lifetime of the Buddha, no one attained the way as a layperson. The reason is that there are so many obstacles that home is not a practice place for studying the buddha way. When we investigate the bodies and minds of those who say that the minds of rulers and the minds of buddha ancestors are the same, we see that their bodies and minds are not the body-mind of buddha dharma.

Dharma Transmission

"Dharma transmission" usually takes place in a private cere-
mony between the teacher and the student in acknowledgment of
the student's maturity and to entrust dharma. Dogen was trans-
mitted dharma from his teacher Rujing upon their first meeting.
But Dogen gave dharma transmission to his students after prac-
ticing with them for a number of years.

All buddha tathagatas who individually transmit inconceivable
dharma, actualizing unsurpassable, complete enlightenment,
have a wondrous art, supreme and unconditioned.

Transmission of buddha dharma in the west and east [India and
China] is no other than transmission of sitting buddha. This is
the pivotal point. Where buddha dharma is not transmitted, zazen is not transmitted. What has been passed on person to person is the essential teaching of zazen alone. Those who have not
intimately received this teaching are not buddha ancestors.

A face-to-face-transmitting buddha transmits to a face-to-
face-transmitting buddha. It is transmitted from vine to vine,

without being cut off. It is transmitted from eye to eye, with the eye open. It is transmitted from face to face, with the face revealed.

—

I first offered incense and bowed formally to Rujing in the abbot's room—Wondrous Light Terrace—on the first day, the fifth month, of the first year of the Baoqing Era of Great Song [1225]. He also saw me for the first time. Upon this occasion he transmitted dharma to me, finger to finger, face to face, and said, "The dharma gate of face-to-face transmission from buddha to buddha, ancestor to ancestor, is actualized now."

Your ability to see buddhas and hear dharma right now is the result of the compassionate continuous practice of each buddha ancestor. Without the one-to-one transmission of buddha ancestors, how could the dharma have reached us today? You should gratefully repay the beneficence of having received one phrase, one dharma. How much more beneficent is the unsurpassed great dharma, the treasury of the true dharma eye? How could you not repay it with gratitude? You should vow to surrender to this day your lifetimes, which could be as immeasurable as the sands of the Ganges.

—

The Great Master Shakyamuni authentically transmitted this splendid method of attaining the way, and all buddha tathagatas of the past, future, and present attain the way by practicing zazen. For this reason it has been transmitted as the front gate. Furthermore, all ancestors in India and China attained the way by practicing zazen. Thus I now teach this front gate to human beings and devas.

—

Shakyamuni Buddha once caused Ananda to ask, "Whose disciples were all buddhas of the past?"

Shakyamuni Buddha answered, "All buddhas of the past are disciples of me, Shakyamuni Buddha."

The presence of all buddhas is like this. To see all buddhas, to succeed in all buddhas, to fulfill the way, is the buddha way of all buddhas. In this buddha way, the document of heritage is always given at the time of transmitting dharma. Those without dharma heritage are people outside the way who believe in spontaneous enlightenment. If the buddha way had not clearly established dharma heritage, how could it have come down to the present?

═

The meaning of the document of heritage is this: you understand the sun, the moon, and the stars and inherit dharma; you attain skin, flesh, bones, and marrow and inherit dharma; you inherit a robe or staff, a pine branch or whisk, an udumbara blossom or a brocade robe; you receive straw sandals or an arched bamboo staff.

At the time of dharma heritage, the document is handwritten with the blood of the finger or the tongue. Or it is handwritten with oil or milk. Every one of these is a document of heritage.

Those who entrust and those who receive this heritage are both the buddhas' heirs. Indeed, whenever buddha ancestors are actualized, dharma heritage is actualized. At the time of actualization, innumerable buddha ancestors arrive without expectation and receive dharma without seeking. Those who inherit dharma are all buddha ancestors.

═

From Shakyamuni Buddha [and Mahakashyapa, the First Ancestor of the Zen lineage] through Huineng there are thirty-four ancestors. The succession of buddhas and ancestors is all handed down in the same way that Mahakashyapa met the Tathagata and the Tathagata attained Mahakashyapa.

In the same way that Shakyamuni Buddha studied with Kashyapa Buddha, masters and disciples exist to this day. In this way the treasury of the true dharma eye has been handed down from person to person. The essential life of buddha dharma is just this authentic transmission. Because buddha dharma is authentically transmitted in this way, it is the direct succession of entrusting.

This being so, the function, the essence, of the buddha way is present with nothing lacking. This has been transmitted from India to China for eighteen thousand miles. It has been transmitted from Buddha's lifetime to the present day for more than two thousand years.

⸺

When Linji was about to pass away, he entrusted Sansheng,* who would later become Zen Master Huiran, and said, "After I pass away, do not let my treasury of the true dharma eye be extinguished."

Sansheng said, "How can I let your treasury of the true dharma eye be extinguished?"

Linji said, "If someone asks you about it, how would you respond?"

Sansheng shouted.

Linji said, "Who would have guessed that my treasury of the true dharma eye has reached as far as this blind donkey and perished?"

Continuous Practice

Although each moment of practice actualizes enlightenment, practice does not end there but continues endlessly without a gap. It even continues beyond one's lifetime.

Continuous practice that actualizes itself is no other than your continuous practice right now. The now of this practice is not originally possessed by the self. The now of this practice does not come and go, enter and depart. The word "now" does not exist before continuous practice. The moment when it is actualized is called "now." This being so, your continuous practice of this day is a seed of all buddhas and the practice of all buddhas. All buddhas are actualized and sustained by your continuous practice.

Blossoms opening and leaves falling now are the actualization of continuous practice.

Great Teacher Shakyamuni Buddha was engaged in continuous practice in the deep mountains from the time he was nineteen years old. At age thirty, after practicing continuously, he attained the way simultaneously with all sentient beings on the great earth. Until he was in his eighties, his practice was sustained in mountains, forests, and monasteries. He did not return to the palace, nor did he claim any property. He wore the same robes and held the same bowls throughout his lifetime. From the time he began teaching, he was not alone even for a day or for an hour. He did not reject offerings from humans and devas. He was patient with the criticism of people outside the way. The lifetime teaching of the Buddha, wearing the pure robes and begging for food, was nothing but continuous practice.

From the time he was the attendant to Mazu until he died, Baizhang, who would later become Zen Master Dazhi, did not let a single day pass without working for the assembly or for others. He graciously modeled *A day of no work is a day of no eating*. When Baizhang was old, he labored just like those in their prime. The assembly was concerned about him, but he did not stop working. At last some students hid the tools from him during the work period. He refused to eat that day, expressing his regret that he could not join the assembly's communal work. This is Baizhang's exemplification of *A day of no work is a day of no eating*. The wind of the Linji School, which is now widely spread in Song China, as well as the wind of other schools, represents the continuous practice of Baizhang's profound teaching.

The continuous practice of buddha ancestors has the great power to awaken both humans and devas, who, however, may not notice that they are helped by it.

In the continuous practice of the way of buddha ancestors, do not be concerned about whether you are a great or a modest hermit, whether you are brilliant or dull. Just forsake name and gain forever and don't be bound by myriad conditions. Do not waste the passing time. Brush off the fire on top of your head. Do not wait for great enlightenment, as great enlightenment is the tea and rice of daily activity. Do not wish for beyond enlightenment, as beyond enlightenment is a jewel concealed in your hair.

If you attain one day of continuous practice, you not only attain the practice of one hundred years but you awaken others for a hundred years.

Continuous practice, day after day, is the most appropriate way of expressing gratitude.

Do not run around after fame and gain in the realm of sound and form. Not to run around is the continuous practice that has been transmitted person to person by buddha ancestors. Mature hermits, beginning hermits, one person, or half a person, I ask you to throw away myriad matters and conditions and to continuously practice the continuous practice of buddha ancestors.

Zhaozhou, Priest Congshen, who would later become Great Master Zhenji of the Guanyin Monastery, first aroused the way seeking mind at the age of sixty-one. He traveled around, carrying a water gourd and a staff with metal rings on top. He kept telling himself, "I will inquire about dharma of anyone who excels me, even a seven-year-old child. I will teach dharma to anyone who has less understanding, even a hundred-year-old."

Thus he studied and understood Nanquan's way. It was an endeavor of twenty years. Finally, when he was eighty years old, he became abbot of the Guanyin Monastery, east of Zhao Province [Zhaozhou]. After that he guided humans and devas for forty years.

Zhaozhou did not write a single letter of request to donors. The monks' hall* was small and without front or back platforms. Once a leg of a sitting platform broke. He replaced it with a charred stick from the fireplace, tying it on with a rope, and used it for many years. When an officer asked for permission to get a new leg, he did not allow it. Follow the spirit of this old buddha.

Zhaozhou became abbot after receiving dharma transmission in his eighties. This was authentic transmission of the true dharma. People called him Old Buddha. Those who have not yet received true transmission of the dharma are lightweights compared with Zhaozhou. Those of you who are younger than eighty may be more active than Zhaozhou. But how can you younger lightweights be equal to him even in his old age? Keeping this in mind, strive in the path of continuous practice.

During the forty years Zhaozhou taught, he did not store worldly property. There was not a grain of rice in the monastery. So the monks would pick up chestnuts and acorns for food, and they would adjust the mealtime to fit the situation. Indeed, this was the spirit of the dragons and elephants of the past. You should long for such practice.

Monks' actions are endeavor in the cloud hall [monks' hall], bowing in the buddha hall, and cleansing in the washhouse.

Further, putting palms together, greeting, burning incense, and boiling water are all right actions. It is not replacing the tail with the head but replacing the head with the head, replacing the mind with the mind, replacing the buddha with the buddha, and replacing the way with the way. This is the right-action-path limb.*

EXPRESSION

Intimate Language

*For Dogen, intimate means direct, close, without separation and
without intermediary words and concepts. Silence and gesture are
part of direct communication.*

When you encounter a [true] person, you invariably hear intimate language and speak intimate language. When you know
yourself, you know intimate action. Thus buddha ancestors can
thoroughly actualize this intimate heart and intimate language.
Know that where there are buddha ancestors, intimate language
and intimate action are immediately manifest. *Intimate* means
close and inseparable. There is no gap. Intimacy embraces
buddha ancestors. It embraces you. It embraces the self. It embraces action. It embraces generations. It embraces merit. It
embraces intimacy.

When intimate language encounters an intimate person, the
buddha eye sees the unseen. Intimate action is not known by
self or other, but the intimate self alone knows it. Each intimate
other goes beyond understanding. Since intimacy surrounds
you, it is fully intimate, half intimate.

Priest Daokai,* who would later become abbot of Mount Dayang, asked Touzi* [Yiqing], "It is said that the thoughts and words of buddha ancestors are everyday tea and rice. Besides this, are there any words or phrases for teaching?"

Touzi said, "Tell me, when the emperor issues a decree in his territory, does he depend upon [ancient] Emperors Yu, Tang, Yao, or Shun?"*

As Daokai was about to open his mouth, Touzi covered it with his whisk. "While you were thinking, you've already received thirty blows."

Daokai was then awakened. He bowed deeply and began to leave.

Touzi said, "Wait, reverend."

Daokai did not turn around, and Touzi said, "Have you reached the ground of no-doubt?"

Daokai covered his ears with his hands and left.

Yunju,* Great Master Hongjue, was asked by an imperial minister who brought an offering, "The World-Honored One had intimate language, and Mahakashyapa did not conceal it. What was the World-Honored One's language?"

Yunju said, "Your Excellency."

"Yes," he responded.

Yunju asked, "Do you understand it?"

The minister said, "No, I don't."

Yunju said, "If you don't understand it, the World-Honored One had intimate language. If you understand it, Mahakashyapa did not conceal it."

The intimate language spoken of here was put forth not only

by Shakyamuni Buddha, the World-Honored One, but also by all buddha ancestors. When there is the World-Honored One, there is intimate language. When there is intimate language, Mahakashyapa does not conceal it. Since there are hundreds and thousands of world-honored ones, there are hundreds and thousands of Mahakashyapas. Study this point without fail, as if cutting through what is impossible to cut through. Investigate it in detail little by little, hundreds and thousands of times, instead of trying to understand it all at once. Do not assume that you understand it right away. Yunju was already a world-honored one, so he had intimate language, and Mahakashyapa did not conceal it. But do not regard the minister's response to Yunju as intimate language.

⟅⟆

An old buddha [Hongzhi Zhengjiao*] said, "Reach over to grasp what's there, and bring its workings right here."

When you take on sustaining this, all things, bodies, actions, and buddhas become intimate with you. These actions, things, bodies, and buddhas are simply covered [immersed] in acceptance. Because they are simply covered in acceptance, through acceptance they are just dropped away.

The covered eye is the radiance of one hundred grass tips; do not be swayed [into thinking] that it does not see one thing, does not see a single matter. The covered eye reaches this thing and that thing. Throughout journeys, while taking on coming and going, or while leaving and entering by the same gate, nothing is hidden in the entire world, and so the World-Honored One's intimate language, intimate realization, intimate practice, and intimate entrustment are present.

⟅⟆

Know that the World-Honored One has two methods of guiding—noble silence and noble speech. All of those who enter the way with either of these methods are like a good horse that runs upon seeing a shadow of the whip.

───

The World-Honored One has intimate language, intimate practice, and intimate realization. But ignorant people think *intimate* means that which is known by the self and not by others. Those east and west, past and present, who think and speak this way are not following the buddha way. If what they think were true, those who do not study would have much intimacy, while those who study would have little intimacy. Would those who study extensively have no intimacy? What about those who have the celestial eye, celestial ear, dharma eye, dharma ear, buddha eye, or buddha ear? Would they have no intimate language or intimate heart?

───

Zhaozhou, Great Master Zhenji, asked a newly arrived monk, "Have you been here before?"

The monk said, "Yes, I have been here."

Zhaozhou said, "Have some tea."

Later he asked another monk, "Have you been here before?"

The monk said, "No, I have not been here."

Zhaozhou said, "Have some tea."

The temple director then asked Zhaozhou, "Why do you say 'Have some tea' to someone who has been here and 'Have some tea' to someone who has not?"

Zhaozhou said, "Director."

"Yes?" replied the Director.

Zhaozhou said, "Have some tea."

‗

When you are already a speechless person, how do you encounter one, how do you speak with one? Investigate in this way and thoroughly study someone who is speechless.

‗

A number of mistaken people think and say that speech and movement are temporary phenomena, while silence and stillness are real. To speak in this way is not buddha dharma. This is a conjecture by those who have heard the scriptures of Brahma* and Indra. How should buddha dharma be determined by movement or stillness? Investigate thoroughly whether buddha dharma does or does not have movement or stillness, whether buddha dharma touches movement or stillness or is touched by movement or stillness. Latecomers to study nowadays should not be lax in this investigation.

Paradox and Poetic Expression

Dogen was an extraordinarily inventive teacher. This can be seen in his creative, perplexing, and poetic use of language, where he would use ordinary words in unusual ways to help the thinking mind leap past itself to realization.

———————————————

Bodhisattvas who study the way, open your minds to mountains flowing and to water not flowing.

⸗

Water is not just earth, water, fire, wind, space, or consciousness. Water is not blue, yellow, red, white, or black. Water is not form, sound, smell, taste, a touchable, or an object of mind. But water as earth, water, fire, wind, and space actualizes itself.

⸗

Because green mountains walk, they are permanent. Although they walk more swiftly than the wind, someone in the mountains does not notice or understand it.

⸗

If you doubt mountains' walking, you do not know your own walking; it is not that you do not walk but that you do not know

164

or understand your own walking. Since you do know your own walking, you should fully know the green mountains' walking.

⸺

Walking forward does not obstruct walking backward. Walking backward does not obstruct walking forward. This is called the mountains' flow and the flowing mountains.

⸺

There is walking, there is flowing, and there is a moment when a mountain gives birth to a mountain child. Because mountains are buddha ancestors, buddha ancestors appear in this way.

⸺

A billion worlds and innumerable lands can be found in a mountain. There are mountains suspended in form; there are mountains suspended in emptiness.

⸺

There is no muscle in the eye. There is no pigment in the paints. This is emancipation right here. As emancipation is not a matter of time, it is not concerned with a discussion of a certain moment or instant. Taking up this understanding, make earth, water, fire, and air your vital activity; make mind, consciousness, and wisdom your great death. In this manner, the activities of the [buddha] house have been passed on with spring, autumn, winter, and summer as furnishings [essentials].

⸺

Taking up a flower and blinking are both the fundamental point actualized by obscured eyes and flowers in the sky. That the treasury of the true dharma eye, the wondrous heart of nirvana, has been authentically transmitted without a gap is called obscured eyes and flowers in the sky.

⸺

The Tathagata says, "When clouds fly the moon moves, and when a boat goes the shore moves." In this way the moon travels when the clouds move, and the shore moves when the boat goes. The meaning of these words is that clouds and moon travel at the same time; they walk together with no beginning or end, no before or after. The boat and the shore travel at the same time; they walk together without starting or stopping, without floating or turning.

⸺

Go away with no string on your straw sandals.

⸺

When the sky flies away, the bird flies away. When the bird flies away, the sky flies away. When you speak about the investigation of flying, it is right here. This is the point of steadfast sitting. Even if you go myriad miles, it is right here.

⸺

The vast sky does not hinder the vast sky. Just as the vast sky does not hinder the vast sky from flying, white clouds do not hinder white clouds. White clouds fly with no hindrance. White clouds' flying does not hinder the vast sky's flying. Not hindering others is not hindering self.

⸺

Here is one vital path for getting up: "One who falls to the ground uses the sky to stand up. One who falls to the sky uses the ground to stand up." Without being thus, you can never get up. This has always been the way with all buddhas and ancestors.

⸺

The withered tree spoken of by buddha ancestors is the understanding of the ocean drying up. The ocean drying up is the tree withering. The tree withering encounters spring. The immovability of the tree is its witheredness. The mountain trees, ocean trees, and sky trees right now are all withered trees. That which sprouts buds is a dragon singing in a withered tree. Those who embrace it one hundredfold, one thousandfold, and one myriadfold are descendants of the withered tree.

$$=$$

A tree with no roots, the ground where no light or shade falls, and a valley where no shouts echo are no other than the actualized expressions of the dream within a dream. This is neither the realm of humans nor of heavenly beings and cannot be judged by ordinary people. Who could doubt that a dream is enlightenment, since it is not within the purview of doubt? Who could recognize this dream, since it is not related to recognition? Since unsurpassable enlightenment is unsurpassable enlightenment, so the dream is called a dream.

$$=$$

Know that the buddhas in the three times* are buddhas who remain and listen to the dharma expounded by flames. The transformative function of this single phrase cannot be traced in a linear manner. If you try to trace it, the arrowhead and the shaft will crush each other. Flames definitely expound dharma for the buddhas of the three times. With bits and pieces of red heart, an iron tree blossoms and the world becomes fragrant.

$$=$$

The Body Born before the Parents

The village I finally reach
deeper than the deep mountains
indeed
the capital
where I used to live!

$$=$$

Closing the Furnace, the First Day of the Third Month

A painted circle comes around to spring.
Opening and closing in accord with the season
     is like you painting.
Stack charcoal, look at the ash, and add snow.
I call it a red furnace.

═══

A plantain has earth, water, fire, air, and emptiness, as well as
mind, consciousness, and wisdom as its roots, stems, branches,
leaves, flowers, fruits, colors, and forms. Accordingly, the plantain wears the autumn wind and is torn in the autumn wind. We
know that it is pure and clear and that not a single particle is
excluded.

═══

The paints for painting rice cakes are the same as those used for
painting mountains and waters. For painting mountains and
waters, blue and red paints are used; for painting rice cakes, rice
flour is used. Thus they are painted in the same way, and they
are examined in the same way.

═══

At the moment of attaining the way, green mountains and white
snow are painted on countless scrolls. Motion and stillness are
nothing but a painting. Our endeavor at this moment is brought
forth entirely from a painting.

═══

When a buddha is painted, not only a clay altar or lump of earth is
used but the thirty-two marks, a blade of grass, and the cultivation
of wisdom for incalculable eons are used. As a buddha has been
painted on a single scroll in this way, all buddhas are painted buddhas, and all painted buddhas are actual buddhas.

Verse Commentaries

Dogen's Chinese-style poems include commentaries on ancient Zen dialogues as cases of study. They are commonly called "koans." In this style of teaching, he presents a koan in Chinese, followed by his comment in verse.

Shigong,* who would later become Zen Master Huizang of Fu Region, asked his younger dharma brother Xitang,* who would later become Zen Master Zhizang, "Do you know how to grasp space?"

Xitang said, "Yes, I do."

Shigong said, "How do you grasp it?"

Xitang stroked the air with his hand.

Shigong said, "You don't know how to grasp space."

Xitang responded, "How do you grasp it, elder brother?"

Shigong poked his finger in Xitang's nostril and pulled.

Xitang grunted in pain and said, "You're killing me! You're pulling off my nose."

Shigong said, "You can grasp it now."

Dogen's commentary:

> Whose tree stands between these two?
> Somewhere in the east, west, south, and north,
> two brothers meet and speak of their parent's [master's]
> labor.
> One grasps the earth, the other pulls the sky.

—

Dongshan, who would later become High Ancestor Great Master Wuben, studied with his teacher Yunyan, Great Priest, Early Ancestor. Dongshan asked Yunyan, "Who can hear insentient beings speak dharma?"

Yunyan said, "Insentient beings hear insentient beings speak dharma."

Dongshan asked, "Do you hear it, sir?"

Yunyan said, "If I heard it, you could not hear me speak dharma."

Dongshan responded: "Being so, I don't hear you speak dharma."

Yunyan replied, "You haven't been hearing me speak dharma. How could you hear insentient beings speak dharma?"

Dongshan responded by presenting this poem:

> How splendid! How wondrous!
> Inconceivable! Insentient beings speak dharma.
> The ears never hear it—
> only the eyes.

Dogen's commentary:

Only the insentient know the dharma they speak of,
just as walls, grass, and trees know spring.
Ordinary and sacred are not hemmed in by boundaries,
nor are mountains and rivers; sun, moon, or stars.

⸻

Once, Caoshan* was asked by a monk, "When it is hot, where should we go to escape the heat?"

Caoshan said, "Escape into the cauldron on burning charcoal."

The monk said, "How do you escape into the cauldron on burning charcoal?"

Caoshan said, "No suffering can reach there."

Dogen's commentary:

Autumn slowly approaches, moonlight's chilly,
fireflies keep chasing the fiery star.*
Once again we will walk in a circle before the burning
    furnace.
Clouds come to the mountain peak, water emerges in a jar.

Poems on Various Themes

Some of Dogen's poems were written in China in his formative years. They were given to literary locals who perhaps invited Dogen for a meal or an overnight stay. We present four such poems, followed by one given to a Japanese samurai government official. Many other poems, some of which are included here, were written during his personal retreat in a mountain hermitage.

Given to a Zen Person

Buddha ancestors are originally right here.
Deep autumn, boat edges are barely seen.
In the cold night, the line of geese is easily broken.
Right and left filled with mist.

≈

Response to Graduate Wen Ben *

The path of delusion runs in front of a decayed tree and
  boulder.
Why borrow a horse and return a cow?
Don't be anxious to plow an idle field.

Hurl away confusion and look toward a distant mountain.

～

Given to Imperial Attendant Wang*

The world is boundless, everything expands and contracts.
Who can arrive without being deluded?
The Iron Bull dams up the River of Heaven.
Vairochana above trails the bottom of your feet.

～

Given to Chengzhong*

The great way has no wheel tracks
but east, west, south, and north—sages can be found.
Though they walk with bare feet, others don't know them:
empty bellies frightened of sesame tea.

～

Given to Sukemitsu Yu* on His Return from Dazai-fu*

When your whole body turns, seeing nowhere else,
it steps forward and backward—three, three—without
    ceasing.
Is there anything beyond this in the ancestral gate?
One vast sky, the moon floats westward.

～

During Retreat

Intimate with everything I see,
walking, sitting, and lying down are truth itself.
If someone asks the inner meaning:
"The treasury of the dharma eye in a speck of dust."

～

During Retreat

Last night the wooden person cut free from its roots.
The bare pillar and lantern long for their beloved.
Companions in the way, realize the realm far beyond,
don't cloud the universe with confusion!

～

Secluded in the Mountains

How pathetic, the shape of an aged person!
My ears and eyes have grown unclear.
Still, there is something hard to throw out yet easy to
    paint—
valley sounds in a grass hut on a rainy autumn night.

～

Secluded in the Mountains

The evening bell rings the moon and raises lanterns.
Monks sit in the hall and quietly observe emptiness.
Having fortunately received the three robes, they now
    sow seeds.
How wonderful, their ripening in just one mind!

～

Secluded in the Mountains

The ancestor's way brought from the west, I transmit east.
Polishing the moon, plowing the cloud, I long for the
    ancient wind.
How can the world's red dust slip into this thatched hut
deep in the mountains on a snowy night?

～

Snow and more snow, one thousand, ten thousand miles,
flake after flake, not the same, not different.
Seeking song, seeking dance, the universe is new.
Burying the moon, burying the clouds, the fire pit
 vanishes.
Five petals and six blossoms accord with time, accord with
 the season.
Not fearing winter's freezing and the year's cold end,
the valley pine and mountain bamboo speak with empty
 hearts.

———

Buddha's Enlightenment

When the morning star is captured, the world turns crimson,
the eyeball thunders, crushing the vast sky.
Upholding attainment of the way in the Saha World,
he thoroughly faces the wind of spring's wooden dipper.

———

Death Poem

Fifty-four years lighting up the sky.
A quivering leap smashes a billion worlds.
Hah! The whole body looks for nothing.
Living, I plunge into Yellow Springs.*

On His Portrait

It seems that some of Dogen's advanced students had artists paint his portrait and then asked Dogen to add a poem to the paintings. These poems may be seen as Dogen's self-image as well as encouragement for his students and dharma descendants.

Splattering salt and soy sauce,
I try to cook.
Satisfied with gruel and rice,
I wash my bowls.
May it remain so.
Do not say heaven and earth are just one finger,
or myriad things just one horse.
How is it after all?
Wherever the eye reaches is a fist
crushing the empty sky, dripping blood.
Wherever the fist reaches is an eye
seeing through its surroundings—
its muscle is long.

Sun face, moon face is the way.
Buddha face, ancestor face is the way.
Encountering is expression—
expression encountering.
Right here is clarity itself,
the top of the head just here from the beginning.
The way and the painting emerge together,
realization and the morning sky are one enlightenment.
Who speaks of a harmonious mind?
Simply say, "Just this!"

━

For thousands of yards, the cold lake soaks up the color of
    the sky.
Evening quiet: a fish of brocade scales reaches the bottom,
then flits this way and that; an arrow notch splits.
Endless water surface, moonlight brilliant.

━

This autumn, a fresh clear spirit covers the old mountain
    man.
The donkey stares at the sky ceiling; a floating moon
    glows white.
Nothing approaches. Nothing else included.
Buoyant, I let myself go—filled with gruel, filled with rice.
Lively flapping from head to tail,
sky above, sky beneath; cloud self, water origin.

━

If you call me not knowing and not understanding,
that is correct.
If you don't call me not knowing and not understanding,
that is not correct.

How do you call me? Say it now.
Just call me a child of Tiantong.

Notes

Macrons are used only in the notes proper, not in the reference terms, which are taken from the main text.

p. 3 *Rujing:* Tiantong Rujing, 1163–1228, China. Dharma heir of Xuedou Zhijian, Caodong School. Abbot of Qingliang Monastery, Jiankang (Jiangsu); Ruiyan Monastery, Tai Region (Zhejiang); and Jingci Monastery, Hang Region (Zhejiang). In 1225 he became abbot of the Jingde Monastery, Mount Tiantong, Ming Region (Zhejiang), where he transmitted dharma to Dōgen.

buddha: An awakened person.

dharma: 1. Ultimate law, reality, or truth. 2. Teaching of truth; one of the three treasures. 3. A thing, all things or phenomena.

sangha: A practicing community of dharma.

Eisai: Myōan Eisai, 1141–1215, Japan. Went to China in 1168 and brought back Tiantai texts. Made a second visit to China between 1185 and 1191 to study Zen. Dharma heir of Xuan Huaichang, Linji School. Author of *On Raising Zen and Protecting the Nation.* Founded Jufuku Monastery in Kamakura and Kennin Monastery in Kyōto. Regarded as founder of the Rinzai School, the Japanese form of the Linji School.

Linji School: One of the Five Schools of Chinese Zen Buddhism.

Regards Linji Yixuan as founder. A Japanese form of the Linji School is the Rinzai School.

Myozen: Butsuju Myōzen, 1184–1225, Japan. Dharma heir of Myōan Eisai. As abbot of the Kennin Monastery, Kyōto, he taught Rinzai Zen to Dōgen. He took Dōgen to China but died at the Tiantong Jingde Monastery during his study.

Song China: Song Dynasty, 960–1279.

p. 5 *Buddha:* 1. Shākyamuni Buddha. 2. Other enlightened beings described in scriptures.

p. 6 *deva:* Celestial being, in the highest of the six paths of transmigration. Dharma teaching is often given to humans and devas.

buddha ancestors: A buddha is an enlightened one. An ancestor is an earlier teacher of the dharma lineage who inherits and transmits dharma.

p. 8 *Shakyamuni Buddha:* Ca. 566–ca. 486 B.C.E., according to Western and Indian scholarship. The founding teacher of Buddhism who taught in the plain along the Ganges, central to eastern part of northern India. In the Mahāyāna Buddhist tradition, the Buddha's enlightenment simultaneously with the awakening of all sentient beings is emphasized. According to the Zen tradition, he transmitted dharma to Mahākāshyapa, the First Ancestor.

samadhi: Serene and stable state of body and mind in meditation.

p. 9 *tathagatas:* Tathāgata literally means "one who has thus gone," "one who has thus come," or "one who has come from thusness." Honorific name for Shākyamuni Buddha, also indicating buddhas in general.

receptive samadhi: The buddhas' realizing and utilizing the joy of samādhi. Contrasted with the aspect of extending samādhi to help other beings.

Mazu: Mazu Daoyi, 709–788, China. Dharma heir of Nanyue Huairang, Nanyue Line. Taught at Kaiyuan Monastery, Zhongling

(Jiangxi). Along with Shitou Xiqian, considered one of the two great jewels of Zen in his time. Had 139 enlightened disciples and made the Nanyue Line of the Southern School flourish. Initiated the Zen tradition of "recorded sayings"—collections of informal dialogues and lectures.

Nanyue: Nanyue Huairang, 677–744, China. Studied fifteen years with Sixth Ancestor Huineng and became his heir along with Qingyuan Xingsi. The teaching lineages derived from Nanyue and Qingyuan became the main streams of the Chinese Zen tradition.

p. 10 *koan:* 1. Fundamental point, first principle, truth that is experienced directly. 2. An exemplary story pointing to this realization. 3. A case that is used to lead students to experience this realization. Dōgen uses this word mainly in the first sense.

p. 11 *Mount Huangmei:* A mountain where Fifth Ancestor Hongren taught. Later called Mount Wuzu (Mount Fifth Ancestor), Qi Region (Hubei).

Hongren: Daman Hongren, 602–675, China. Dharma heir of Fourth Ancestor Dayi Daoxin. As Fifth Chinese Ancestor of the Zen School, taught at Mount Huangmei, Qi Region (Hubei). He had two outstanding students, Shenxiu and Huineng. Hongren is regarded as the one who established the Dongshan (East Mountain) School (Tōzan Shū), in contrast to the contemporary Niutou School. (Not to be confused with Dongshan Liangjie's Caodong School.)

kashaya: A patched robe worn over one shoulder by a Buddhist monk or nun. Represents a monk or nun.

p. 13 *World-Honored One:* One of the ten honorific names of the Buddha. Often meaning Shākyamuni Buddha.

p. 14 *bodhi tree:* The tree under which the Buddha attained enlightenment.

dharma wheel: Unfolding teaching of the Buddha.

thusness: Reality itself, which is limitless and undivided.

ocean mudra samadhi: A state of meditation that is as vast and dynamic as an ocean.

p. 16 *stupa:* Shrine or tower for relics.

sutra: An Indian Buddhist scripture that takes the form of a discourse by the Buddha as heard and verified by one of his disciples.

p. 17 *dharani [magic]:* Literally, "maintaining all." 1. Magical verses chanted in Esoteric Buddhism. 2. In Dōgen's usage, bowing and offering respect to the teacher, which is no other than bowing to the Buddha.

Indra: Originally a Vedic deity. Regarded in Buddhism as a main guardian deity of dharma. Resides in the Heaven of Thirty-three Devas (Tushita Heaven) above Mount Sumeru.

King of the Empty Eon: There are the four stages in a world cycle: becoming, abiding, decaying, and empty. The buddha who appears in the Empty Eon is called the King of the Empty Eon or King of Emptiness. Regarded as symbol of the original face.

p. 21 *five organs:* Ancient Chinese classification: heart, kidney, lung, liver, and spleen.

six sub-organs: Ancient Chinese classification: colon, small intestine, stomach, gallbladder, bladder, and three "jiaos" (an area that includes the lower heart and upper stomach).

Linji: Linji Yixuan, d. 867, China. Dharma heir of Huangbo Xiyun, Nanyue Line. Taught at Linji Monastery, Zhen Region (Hebei). Known for his shouting and dynamic teaching. Regarded as founder of Linji School, one of the Five Schools of Chinese Zen.

Huangbo: Huangbo Xiyun, d. 850, China. Dharma heir of Baizhang Huaihai, Nanyue Line. Taught at a mountain at Zhongling (Jiangxi), which he named Huangbo after his place of ordination. He was known for striking with a stick as a teaching device. Linji Yixuan was one of his successors.

p. 23 *Agama Sutra:* Early Buddhist sūtra(s). Many of the Sanskrit versions were translated into Chinese.

p. 27 *Mahakashyapa:* A senior disciple of Shākyamuni Buddha who was engaged in rigorous ascetic practice. Regarded as the First Ancestor of the Zen School.

nirvana: The state of enlightenment attained by Shākyamuni Buddha or by any other buddha. Literally, "extinction of fire," meaning extinction of desires. It often indicates liberation from the cycle of birth, death, and rebirth. In Mahāyāna Buddhism, nirvāna is viewed as not separate from birth and death, as opposed to extinction of birth and death. In Dōgen's usage, nondualistic experience.

Seven Original Buddhas: Succession of six mythological buddhas before Shākyamuni Buddha, plus Shākyamuni Buddha.

Bodhidharma: Ca. fifth–sixth century, India and China. Regarded as the Twenty-eighth Indian Ancestor and the First Chinese Ancestor in the Zen tradition. Dharma heir of Prajñātāra, India. According to legend, he had a dialogue with Emperor Wu of the southern kingdom of Liang, but Wu did not understand him. Then he went to the northern kingdom of Wei and sat at Shaolin Temple, Shaoshi Peak, Mount Song (Henan). He taught Huike, Daoyu, Daofu, and the nun Zongchi.

p. 28 *Huineng:* Dajian Huineng, 638–713, China. Sold firewood for a living. At age twenty-four he joined Fifth Ancestor Hongren's community. After cleaning rice for eight months, he secretly received dharma transmission from Hongren and ran from angry senior monks to the south. Hid in a hunter's house for four years and then became a monk. Taught at Baolin Monastery, Caoxi, Shao Region (Guangdong). While Hongren's senior student, Shenxiu, emphasized gradual enlightenment in northern China, Huineng emphasized immediate enlightenment. As a teacher, he produced a group of excellent students who transmitted his teaching, called the "Southern School of Zen."

Gautama: Shākyamuni Buddha's family name.

p. 29 *Jinling:* The capital city of southern kingdoms in China. Present-day Nanjing (Jiangsu).

Wu: Founder of the southern kingdom of Liang. Reigned 502–549. Regarded as one who had a dialogue with Bodhidharma upon his arrival in China.

p. 30 *Luoyang:* The capital city of the Wei Kingdom (Henan).

Shaolin Temple of Mount Song: Also called Shaolin Peak (Henan), China, where Bodhidharma sat facing the wall for nine years.

Emperor [Xiaoming] of Wei: The ruler of Wei when Bodhidharma arrived in the northern country of Wei was Emperor Xiaoming (reigned 516–528).

Huike: Dazu Huike, 487–593. The Second Ancestor of Chinese Zen. According to legend, when he visited Bodhidharma at Shaolin Temple and asked for instruction, Bodhidharma would not reply. Finally, while standing in the snow, Huike cut off his arm and gave it to Bodhidharma as a sign of his sincerity. Thus, he received instruction.

p. 32 *Akshobhya Buddha's:* Of the Buddha of the Eastern Realm.

five skandhas: Five streams of body and mind: (1) form (matter), (2) feeling, (3) perception, (4) inclination, (5) discernment. What is commonly seen as a self is explained as a continuous interaction of these elements, and not a fixed and independent reality.

p. 33 *Xiangyan:* Xiangyan Zhixian, d. 898. Guiyang School. Ordained by Baizhang Huaihai and studied with Guishan Lingyou. Left Guishan and was enlightened by the sound of a pebble striking bamboo while he was sweeping at a graveyard. Became dharma heir of Guishan and taught at Xiangyan Monastery, Deng Region (Henan).

Guishan: Guishan Lingyou, 771–853, China. Dharma heir of Baizhang Huaihai, Nanyue Line. Along with his costudent Huangbo Xiyun, Guishan was a renowned Zen teacher of Tang Dynasty China. Taught at Mount Gui, Tan Region (Hunan). He had forty-one room-entering (senior) students, one of whom was Yangshan Huiji. Guishan and Yangshan are regarded as cofounders of the Guiyang School, the first of the Five Schools of Chinese Zen to come into existence.

Zhao: Hutou Zhao, ca. ninth–tenth century. A student of Xiang-yan Zhixian. Biography unknown.

p. 35 *Fada:* Ca. seventh–eighth century, China. Originally a prac-titioner of chanting the *Lotus Sutra*. Dharma heir of Sixth An-cestor Huineng. Taught at Nanhua Monastery, Shao Region (Guangdong).

Lotus Sutra: "Sūtra of Wondrous Dharma Blossoms." Full of para-bles and poetic imagery, this scripture is one of the most revered in the Mahāyāna canon. Other sūtras are considered provisional teachings, as opposed to the "complete" or supreme teaching of the *Lotus*. Unique to this sūtra are the teachings of One Vehicle and of Buddha's enlightenment from the beginningless past.

p. 37 *Heart Sutra:* A short sutra, it is the most frequently recited scripture in Mahāyāna tradition, expounding prajñā that sees all things as shūnyatā, or without boundary.

Zhaozhou: Zhaozhou Congshen, 778–897, China. He aroused as-piration for enlightenment at age sixty-one. Dharma heir of Nanquan Puyuan, Qingyuan Line. Taught for forty years at Guanyin Monastery, Zhaozhou (Hebei). A great many of his sayings and anecdotes about him are used as kōans, including the kōan "mu," about a dog's buddha nature.

p. 39 *Kashyapa Matanga:* Ca. first century C.E. A monk from cen-tral India who introduced Buddhism to China together with Dharmaratna in 67 C.E., during the reign of Emperor Xiao-ming of the Later Han Dynasty.

p. 40 *Qingyuan Xingsi:* d. 740, China. Dharma heir of Sixth An-cestor Huineng. Abbot of Jingju Monastery, Mount Qingyuan, Ji Region (Jiangxi). Regarded as founder of the Qingyuan Line, from which the Caodong, Yunmen, and Fayan schools derived.

Fayan School: The lineage of Fayan Wenyi (885–958). One of the Five Schools of Chinese Zen Buddhism.

Guiyang School: One of the Five Schools of Chinese Zen Bud-dhism. Regards Guishan Lingyou and Yangshan Huiji as founders.

Caodong School: The dharma lineage derived from Dongshan Liangjie. Sometimes his successor Caoshan Benji is regarded as cofounder. There is also a theory that the name of this school comes from "Caoxi," where Sixth Ancestor Huineng lived, plus "Dongshan." One of the Five "Houses" of Zen in China. Dōgen brought this teaching and is regarded as founder of its Japanese form, the Sōtō School. *Sōtō* is a Japanese transliteration of *Caodong*.

Yunmen School: A lineage from Yunmen Wenyan (864–949). One of the Five Schools of Zen in China.

p. 41 *Doctrinal School:* Also, Scriptural School. Zen Buddhist way of naming some other schools of Buddhism whose teaching is based on specific sūtras or treatises. Zen Buddhists explain that Zen teaching is based directly on Shākyamuni Buddha's enlightenment without depending upon any particular sūtras. This is described as "transmission outside of scriptures."

Precept School: One of the Thirteen Schools of Buddhism in China, based on the Mahāyāna system of precepts. Nanshan Daoxuan (596–667) is regarded as founder.

Nanshan: See the previous note.

Tiantai: Tiantai School. Established by Zhiyi at Mount Tiantai, Tai Region (Zhejiang), China, in the sixth century C.E. Based on Zhiyi's classification of the entire canon. Central to this school are the *Lotus Sūtra* and the meditation practices of *shamatha* (cessation of wavering mind) and *vipashyanā* (visualization). Dōgen was first ordained as a monk at Mount Hiei, center of the Tendai School, the Japanese form of the Tiantai School.

Yoga School: A Chinese school of Buddhism based on the teaching of Yogācāra, established by Asanga and Vasubandhu of Gandhara in the fourth century. This teaching is often characterized as "mind only."

Amoghavajra: 705–774, a monk from India. Arrived in Luo-yang, China, and studied with Vajrabodhi. Brought Vajrayāna scriptures from Ceylon (present-day Sri Lanka) to China and translated them into Chinese. Taught Vajrayāna practice and Yogācāra philosophy.

p. 48 *all-inclusive study of fifteen years:* In the East Asian way of counting the number of years, a partial year is counted as one, and two partial years are also counted as one ($7 + x = 8$; $7 + x + 7 + x = 14 + 1 = 15$).

p. 50 *Ejo:* Koun Ejō, 1198–1280, Japan. After studying Zen with Kakuan of the Japan Daruma School, he became Dōgen's student in 1234 and, later, the first head monk. As the most advanced student, he assisted Dōgen, edited many of his writings, and became his dharma heir. He was appointed the second abbot of the Eihei Monastery by Dōgen in 1253.

p. 60 *Vairochana:* The dharma-body buddha, manifestation of reality of the universe. Literally, illumination buddha.

twelve hours of the day: In ancient East Asia, a day was divided into twelve hours.

p. 62 *bodhisattvas of the ten stages or three classes:* According to the Tiantai and Huayan doctrines, bodhisattvas are classified into forty-two stages based on their maturity. The beginning thirty degrees are called "three classes" (ten stages of abiding, ten stages of practice, ten stages of dedication). The more advanced ten degrees are called the "ten stages." That makes forty stages. There are yet two more stages before becoming a buddha: the stage of enlightenment equal to the Buddha's, and the stage of inconceivable enlightenment.

Mayu: Mayu Baoche, ca. eighth–ninth century, China. Dharma heir of Mazu Daoyi, Nanyue Line. Taught at Mount Mayu, Pu Region (Shanxi).

p. 67 *Yunyan:* Yunyan Tansheng, 782–841, China. Studied with Baizhang Huaihai for twenty years, then became a disciple of Yaoshan Weiyan and inherited dharma from him. Taught at Yunyan, Tan Region (Hunan). Many dialogues are recorded between Yunyan and his dharma and biological brother Daowu Yuanzhi. Dongshan Liangjie, who studied with several famous teachers, regarded the lesser-known Yunyan as his dharma teacher because Yunyan never explained anything directly.

Daowu: Daowu Yuanzhi, 769–835, China. Dharma heir of Yaoshan Weiyan, Qingyuan Line. He traveled for many years to various Zen monasteries and then resided and taught at Mount Daowu, Tan Region (Hunan). He was biological and dharma brother of Yunyan Tansheng. A number of dialogues between them remain and were commented on by Dōgen.

Four Continents: According to sūtras, the world consists of Eight Seas around Mount Sumeru. Four Continents lie in the Eight Seas. Among them, the Great Northern Continent is where inhabitants live for one thousand years and don't know suffering. The Southern Continent is our world on Earth, where we humans live with suffering, but where there is the potential for awakening.

p. 71 *Kennin Monastery:* Founded by Myōan Eisai in Kyōto. Dōgen visited this Rinzai School monastery when Eisai was alive and studied with Myōzen, the successor of Eisai as the second abbot. After his return from China, Dōgen resided there while looking for a place for his own training center.

Medicine Buddha: Bhaishajyarāja, the buddha of healing.

p. 78 *Zhixian [Guanxi]:* Guanxi Zhixian, d. 895, China. Dharma heir of Linji Yixuan, Linji School. Taught at Guanxi, Changsha (Hunan).

Moshan: Moshan Liaoran, ca. ninth century, China. Nun. Dharma heir of Gaoan Dayu, Nanyue Line. Taught at Mount Mo, Yun Region (Jiangxi). She was a prominent female teacher in the early, male-dominated Zen School.

p. 79 *Miaoxin:* Ca. ninth century, China. Nun who was a student of Yangshan Huiji, Guiyang School. Served as director of the guesthouse in Yangshan's monastery.

Yangshan: Yangshan Huiji, 803–887, China. Opposed by his parents, he cut off two fingers to show his determination to become a monk. When young, studied with Baizhang Huaihai. He was like Shāriputra, who gave one hundred answers to ten questions and was called Small Shākyamuni. Attending Guishan Lingyou, he spent three years watching over a buffalo. Became dharma heir of Guishan. Taught at Mount Yang, Yuan Region (Jiangxi). Guiyang School was partly named after him.

p. 80 *Deshan:* Deshan Xuanjian, 780–865, China. He was a well-known commentator of the *Diamond Sūtra* and called himself Diamond King Chou after his family name. Unable to answer a rice-cake seller's simple question, he became a Zen student. Later he became a dharma heir of Longtan Chongxin, Qingyuan Line. Taught at Mount De, Ding Region (Hunan). Known for teaching by shouting and striking his students.

Diamond Sutra: One of the Prajñā Pāramitā scriptures in Mahāyāna Buddhism, expounding the principle of shūnyatā (emptiness) without using the word.

Xinlong Commentary: The *Diamond Sūtra* commentary by Daoyin, of Xinlong Monastery in the capital city of Chang'an, written at the request of Emperor Xian (reigned 846–859) of Tang Dynasty.

Longtan: Longtan Chongxin, ca. eighth–ninth century, China. Dharma heir of Tanhuang Daowu, Qingyuan Line. Lived in a hut in Longtan, Feng Region (Hunan).

p. 83 *Guidelines for Zen Monasteries:* Compiled by Changlu Zongze (eleventh–twelfth century) of the Yunmen School, China. Published in 1103. The oldest extant collection of monastic guidelines, as most of the earlier guidelines, attributed to Baizhang, had been lost. Basis for later monastic guidelines.

Mahayana Indra Net Sutra: Indra's Net Bodhisattva Precepts Sūtra. Mahāyāna sūtra revered for its elucidation of the bodhisattva precepts.

p. 92 *Shitou:* Shitou Xiqian, 700–790, China. Ordained by Sixth

Ancestor Huineng, after whose death he studied with Qingyuan Xingsi and became his dharma heir. As he did zazen continually in a hut built on a rock at Nan Monastery, Mount Heng (Hunan), he was called Priest Rock Head (Shitou). Author of "Merging of One and Many" and "Song of the Grass Hut."

p. 93 *Yaoshan:* Yaoshan Weiyan, 745–828, China. He was an earnest student of the precepts, but when he grew weary of the repetitive observances, he went to study with Shitou Xiqian, Qingyuan Line, and became his dharma heir. Taught at Mount Yao, Feng Region (Hunan).

p. 96 *Faxing Fatai:* Ca. eleventh–twelfth century, China. Dharma heir of Yuanwu Keqin, Linji School. Abbot of Mount Dagui, Tan Region (Hunan).

p. 97 *Saha World:* The cosmos within the reach of Shākyamuni Buddha's teaching. Literally, worlds of endurance, referring to the hardship of inhabitants, which requires the development of patience. Sūtras say that there are a billion such worlds, each consisting of Mount Sumeru and the Four Continents that surround it.

p. 110 *Faxing Monastery:* Situated in Guang Region (Guangdong), China.

Avatamsaka Sutra: A major Mahāyāna sūtra, known for its magnificent cosmic view of all things interreflecting, centering on Vairochana Buddha.

p. 114 *Shenshan:* Shenshan Sengmi, ca. eighth–ninth century, China. Dharma heir of Yunyan Tansheng, Qingyuan Line. Traveled for twenty years with his dharma junior brother Dongshan Liangjie. A number of their dialogues have been recorded. Dongshan's students respectfully called him Dharma Uncle Mi (Sengmi).

Dongshan: Dongshan Liangjie. 807–869, China. Dharma heir of Yunyan Tansheng, Qingyuan Line. Taught at Mount Dong, Rui Region (Jiangxi). Author of "Song of Precious Mirror

Samādhi." Regarded as a founder of the Caodong School, one of the Five Schools of Chinese Zen.

p. 117 *Hironaga Hatano:* Ca. thirteenth century, Japan. Biography unknown. Possibly related to Yoshishige Hatano, the major benefactor of Dōgen in Echizen Province.

p. 119 *Baizhang:* Baizhang Huaihai, 749–814, China. Dharma heir of Mazu Daoyi, Nanyue Line. Many of Huaihai's students from all over built a monastery on Mount Daxiong in Hao Region (Jiangxi). Even when he was older, he always participated in communal labor and is known for his words "A day of no work is a day of no eating." As compiler of the first known Zen monastic guidelines, he contributed greatly to the establishment of monastic practice suited to Chinese seekers.

p. 120 *Kumaralabha:* Originally a Brahman, he became a monk and Nineteenth Ancestor of the Zen tradition in India.

Jayata: Monk from north India. Twentieth Ancestor of the Zen tradition in India.

p. 122 *Keizan Jokin:* 1268–1325, Japan. The first biographical account of Dōgen was written by Keizan Jōkin, who was a dharma successor of Gikai, one of Dōgen's senior students. It appears as a chapter of Keizan's book, *Transmission of Light*, completed forty-seven years after Dōgen's death. Had a great number of followers and founded Yōkō Monastery and Sōji Monastery. He is regarded as the second founder of the Sōtō School.

p. 128 *Dongpo:* Su Dongpo, 1036–1101, China. Renowned poet of Song Dynasty, also a high government official. Lay student of Zhaojue Changzong. Later studied with Foyin Liaoyuan.

Changzong: Zhaojue Changzong, 1025–1091, China. Dharma heir of Huanglong Huinan, Linji School. Taught at Donglin Monastery, Jiang Region (Jiangxi). Teacher of Su Dongpo.

Lingyun: Lingyun Zhiqin, ca. ninth century, China. Studied with Guishan Lingyou, Guiyang School. After practicing for thirty years, had realization upon seeing peach blossoms. Taught at Mount Lingyun, Fu Region (Fujian).

p. 134 *Shariputra:* One of the ten major disciples of the Buddha. Regarded as the best listener among disciples of the Buddha. Many sūtras take the form of the Buddha delivering discourses to him.

Maudgalyayana: One of the ten major disciples of the Buddha. Born to a Brahman family near Rājagriha. Together with his close friend Shāriputra, he became a student of the Buddha. Known for his mastery of miraculous powers.

p. 135 *Pangyun:* 740–808, China. A lay student of Mazu Daoyi, Nanyue Line; also studied with Shitou. Lived in Xiang Region (Hubei) and made his living by making baskets and having his daughter Lingzhao sell them in town. His teachings are found in *Recorded Sayings of Layman Pang*.

p. 136 *Lesser Vehicles:* According to the traditional Mahāyāna Buddhist view, the Buddha's teaching is classified into three ways: the Shrāvaka (listener) Vehicle; the Pratyeka-buddha (solitary awakened one) Vehicle; and the Mahāyāna, or Great Vehicle. The first two are called in a derogatory way the Hīnayāna, or Lesser (Smaller) Vehicles. The Great Vehicle, which emphasizes bringing all sentient beings to enlightenment, is also called the Bodhisattva Vehicle.

p. 140 *Bhaishajyaraja Bodhisattva:* A bodhisattva of healing described in the *Lotus Sūtra*.

p. 141 *Ananda:* A cousin of Shākyamuni Buddha. Became his disciple and attendant. Known as the foremost learner of the Buddha's teaching, who remembered and narrated the sūtras after the Buddha's death. Dharma heir of Mahākāshyapa, he is regarded as the Second Ancestor in the Zen tradition.

p. 144 *Kapilavastu:* Literally, town of Kapila, center for Shākya Clan's Region (present-day central southern Nepal, bordering India). Siddhārtha's father, King Shuddodana, ruled this Re gion. Lumbinī Garden, where Siddhārtha was born, is in the western side of the town.

Mahanaman of Shakya Clan: One of the five monks who practiced with the Buddha after he left the castle. A grandson of King Sim-hahanu. Later he retuned to be a lay practitioner and became king of Kapilavastu while the Buddha was alive.

p. 145 *Emperor Wu of the Liang Dynasty:* See *Wu* for p. 29.

Emperor Yang of the Sui Dynasty: Second emperor of the Sui Dynasty, China. Reigned 604–618.

Emperors Dai and Su: Dai, eighth emperor of the Tang Dynasty, China; reigned 762–779. Su, seventh emperor of the Tang Dynasty, China; reigned 756–762.

p. 146 *Ministers Li and Fang:* Li, ca. ninth century, China, studied Zen with Yaoshan Weiyan, Qingyuan Line. Fang Xuanling, 578–648, China, was prime minister for fifteen years, serving Emperor Tai, second emperor of the Tang Dynasty. Also a historian.

Minister Feng: Also known as Pei Xiu, 797–870, governor of Qiong Region (Sichuan), China; studied Zen with Fayan Qingyuan.

p. 151 *Sansheng:* Sansheng Huiran, ca. ninth–tenth century, China. Linji School. After becoming a dharma heir of Linji Yixuan, visited and studied with Yangshan, Deshan, and Xuefeng. Taught at Sansheng Monastery, Zhen Region (Hebei). Traditionally regarded as the compiler of the *Record of Linji.*

p. 155 *monks' hall:* One of the main buildings of a Zen monastery, where monks reside, engage in zazen, and take morning and midday meals.

p. 156 *right-action-path limb:* One of the eightfold-noble-path limbs of enlightenment, listed among the thirty-seven wings or conditions favorable to enlightenment.

p. 160 *Daokai:* Furong Daokai, 1043–1118, China. Dharma heir of Touzi Yiqing, Caodong School. Also called Dayang. Before he studied Zen, he engaged in Daoist sorcery. He taught at Mount

Dayang, Ying Region (Hubei), and later at Lake Furong (Shandong).

Touzi: Touzi Yiqing, 1032–1083, China. Dharma heir of Dayang Jingxuan, Caodong School. Taught at Mount Touzi, Shu Region (Anhui). Restored the Caodong School.

Emperors Yu, Tang, Yao, or Shun: Legendary emperors of ancient China.

Yunju: Yunju Daoing, d. 902, China. Caodong School. Dharma heir of Dongshan Liangjie. He founded Jenru Monastery on Mount Yunju, Hong Region (Jiangxi), and taught many monks there for more than thirty years.

p. 161 *Hongzhi Zhengjiao:* 1091–1157, China. Dharma heir of Danxia Zichun, Caodong School. As abbot at Mount Tiantong, his monastery flourished with as many as twelve hundred monks in residence. Regarded as leader of "silent-illumination Zen," he was a prolific writer who poetically articulated Caodong meditation practice.

p. 163 *Brahma:* Highest god of Brahmanism. Regarded as one of the former lives of the Buddha, an initial listener of the Buddha's discourse, and a guardian deity who protects Buddhist teachings.

p. 167 *three times:* Past, present, and future.

p. 169 *Shigong:* Shigong Huizang, ca. eighth century, China. Dharma heir of Mazu Daoyi, Nanyue Line. Previously a hunter, he arrived at Mazu's monastery while chasing a deer. Taught at Mount Shigong, Fu Region (Jiangxi).

Xitang: Xitang Zhizang, 735–814, China. Dharma heir of Mazu Daoyi, Nanyue Line. As Mazu commented, "Zang's head is white, Hai's head is black." Zhizang and Baizhang Huaihai were the outstanding students of Mazu.

p. 171 *Caoshan:* Caoshan Benji, 840–901, China. Dharma heir of Dongshan Liangjie. Sometimes regarded as a cofounder of Caodong School along with his teacher Dongshan. Studied Confucianism as a youth; entered Lingshi Monastery in Fuzhou at nineteen. After becoming Dongshan's dharma heir, he started a temple at Mount Cao, Fu Region (Jiangxi). He used Dong-shan's "five ranks" as a method of instruction, thereby widening its use.

fiery star: Mars.

p. 172 *Graduate Wen Ben:* Biography unknown. Exchanged poems with Dōgen in Zhejiang Province, China.

p. 173 *Imperial Attendant Wang:* Biography unknown. Exchanged poems with Dōgen in Zhejiang Province, China.

Chengzhong: Biography unknown. Exchanged poems with Dōgen in Zhejiang Province, China.

Sukemitsu Yu: Biography unknown. A Japanese official working at Dazai-fu.

Dazai-fu: The government administrative headquarters in the western Region, based in Chikuzen Province, Kyūshū Island.

p. 175 *Yellow Springs:* A world of the dead.

Sources and Translation Credits

ABBREVIATIONS

Source books edited by Kazuaki Tanahashi:

BT: Beyond Thinking: A Guide to Zen Meditation, by Zen Master Dogen

EU: Enlightenment Unfolds: The Essential Teachings of Zen Master Dogen

MD: Moon in a Dewdrop: Writings of Zen Master Dogen

TTDE: Treasury of the True Dharma Eye: Zen Master Dogen's Shobo Genzo

Reference book translated by Taigen Dan Leighton and Shohaku Okumura:

DER: Dogen's Extensive Record: A Translation of the Eihei Koroku

Reference book translated by Kazuaki Tanahashi and John Daido Loori:

TDE: The True Dharma Eye: Zen Master Dogen's Three Hundred Koans

All texts quoted in this book are translated by Kazuaki Tanahashi and a cotranslator. The cotranslator's name for each text is shown below.

p. 3 I wrote to . . . : "Journal of My Study in China," EU, p. 3. Norman Fischer.

p. 4 The aspiration . . . : "Body-and-Mind Study of the Way," TTDE, p. 425. Dan Welch.

From the moment . . . : "Seeing the Buddha," TTDE, p. 596. Gaelyn Godwin.

p. 5 You should stop . . . : "Recommending Zazen to All People," TTDE, p. 907. Edward Brown.

Endeavor wholeheartedly . . . : "Valley Sounds, Mountain Colors," TTDE, p. 93. Katherine Thanas.

To arouse the aspiration . . . : "Arousing the Aspiration for the Unsurpassable," TTDE, p. 647. Steve Allen.

In general . . . : "Valley Sounds, Mountain Colors," TTDE, p. 93. Katherine Thanas.

p. 6 Eighty thousand . . . : "Arousing the Aspiration for the Unsurpassable," TTDE, p. 647. Steve Allen.

As soon as you arouse . . . : "Valley Sounds, Mountain Colors," TTDE, p. 90. Katherine Thanas.

To study with mind . . . : "Body-and-Mind Study of the Way," TTDE, p. 422. Dan Welch.

p. 7 Awake or Asleep: MD, p. 213. Brian Unger.

p. 8 This ordinary everyday sitting . . . : "All-Inclusive Study," TTDE, p. 610. Mel Weitsman.

To transcend...: "King of Samadhis," TTDE, p. 667. Norman Fischer.

Shakyamuni Buddha said . . . : Ibid., p. 668.

p. 9 All buddha tathagatas . . . : "On the Endeavor of the Way," TTDE, p. 1. Lewis Richmond.

Mazu of Jiangxi . . . : "Old Mirror," TTDE, p. 219. Lewis Richmond.

p. 10 Even if you obtain . . . : "Informal Talks," EU, p. 57. Michael Wenger.

Sit zazen wholeheartedly . . . : "On the Endeavor of the Way," TTDE, p. 10. Lewis Richmond.

Rules for Zazen: TTDE, p. 579. Dan Welch.

p. 13 On Zazen Practice: MD, p. 13. Brian Unger.

The activity of zazen . . . : "The Point of Zazen," TTDE, p. 313. Michael Wenger.

The Tathagata . . . : "King of Samadhis," TTDE, p. 669. Norman Fischer.

p. 14 When even . . . : "On the Endeavor of the Way," TTDE, p. 5. Lewis Richmond.

Honored practitioners . . . : "Recommending Zazen to All People," TTDE, p. 909. Edward Brown.

In the great way . . . : "Ocean Mudra Samadhi," TTDE, p. 386. Katherine Thanas.

p. 15 Samadhi is . . . : "Seeing the Buddha," TTDE, p. 599. Gaelyn Godwin.

Here is the place . . . : "Actualizing the Fundamental Point," TTDE, p. 32. Robert Aitken.

p. 16 Bowing Formally: MD, p. 214. Brian Unger.

You abandon . . . : "Arousing the Aspiration for the Unsurpassable," TTDE, p. 647. Steve Allen.

p. 17 To bow all the way . . . : "Body-and-Mind Study of the Way," TTDE, p. 428. Dan Welch.

Rujing chanted . . . : "Journal of My Study in China," EU, p. 8. Norman Fischer.

When the emperor . . . : "Thirty-seven Wings of Enlightenment," TTDE, p. 686. Peter Levitt.

The great dharani . . . : "Dharani," TTDE, p. 564. Joan Halifax.

p. 18 When bowing remains . . . : Ibid., p. 566.

p. 19 We will thoroughly . . . : "Donation Request for a Monks' Hall at the Kannondori Monastery," EU, p. 48. Michael Wenger.

If there is . . . : "Instructions for the Tenzo," MD, p. 58. Arnold Kotler.

In performing . . . : Ibid., p. 64.

p. 20 When you prepare . . . : Ibid., p. 56.

During my stay . . . : Ibid., p. 58.

p. 21 The awesome practice . . . : "Washing the Face," TTDE, p. 56. Linda Ruth Cutts.

When Linji was . . . : "Continuous Practice, Part One," TTDE, p. 350. Mel Weitsman.

p. 22 Once when I was . . . : "Power of the Robe," TTDE, p. 134. Blanche Hartman.

p. 23 Know that a kashaya . . . : "Transmitting the Robe," TTDE, p. 146. Jean Selkirk.

If you make patched robes . . . : "On the Endeavor of the Way," TTDE, p. 21. Lewis Richmond.

With this body . . . : "The Reality of All Things," TTDE, p. 521. Lewis Richmond.

p. 24 Once your body . . . : "Dharani," TTDE, p. 567. Joan Halifax.

p. 27 Once, on Vulture Peak . . . : "Face-to-Face Transmission," TTDE, p. 569. Reb Anderson.

p. 28 Within three . . . . : "Plum Blossoms," TTDE, p. 585. Mel Weitsman.

Mountains, rivers . . . : "Udumbara Blossom," TTDE, p. 643. Chozen Bayes and Hogen Bayes.

p. 29 Bodhidharma went . . . : "Continuous Practice, Part Two," TTDE, p. 355. Mel Weitsman.

p. 30 In China after . . . : "On the Endeavor of the Way," TTDE, p. 5. Lewis Richmond.

Finally Huike . . . : "Continuous Practice, Part Two," TTDE, p. 364. Mel Weitsman.

p. 32 Bodhidharma once said . . . : "Twining Vines," TTDE, p. 479. Mel Weitsman.

When Bodhidharma gives . . . : Ibid., p. 483.

p. 33 Once Bodhidharma said . . . . : "Speaking of Mind, Speaking of Essence," TTDE, p. 495. Peter Levitt.

Xiangyan . . . : "Dragon Song," TTDE, p. 638. Mel Weitsman.

p. 34 Spring Snow Night: MD, p. 217. David Schneider. See also DER, p. 628.

p. 35 In China, since . . . : "Dharma Blossoms Turn Dharma Blossoms," TTDE, p. 171. Michael Wenger.

A monk called Fada . . . : Ibid., p. 182.

p. 37 Even one thousand sutras . . . : "Transmitting the Robe," TTDE, p. 144. Jean Selkirk.

Buddha ancestors all . . . : "Space," TTDE, p. 719. Alan Senauke.

Zhaozhou . . . : "Reading a Sutra," TTDE, p. 226. John Daido Loori.

There are no voices . . . .: "Buddha Sutras," TTDE, p. 541. Mel Weitsman.

Both following . . . : "Self-Realization Samadhi," TTDE, p. 697. Mel Weitsman.

p. 38 You receive sutras . . . : "Buddha Sutras," TTDE, p. 540. Mel Weitsman.

Arousing the aspiration . . . : Ibid., p. 537.

A sutra is . . . : "Tathagata's Entire Body," TTDE, p. 665. John Daido Loori.

The sutras are . . . : "Buddha Sutras," TTDE, p. 538. Mel Weitsman.

p. 39 Rujing said . . . : "Journal of My Study in China," EU, p. 4. Norman Fischer.

p. 40 Know that . . . : Ibid.

Bodhidharma went . . . : "On the Endeavor of the Way," TTDE, p. 4. Lewis Richmond.

When the great master . . . : Ibid., p. 11.

p. 41 Rujing said . . . : "Journal of My Study in China," EU, p. 19. Norman Fischer.

Before I formally bowed . . . : "The Buddha Way," TTDE, p. 507. Peter Levitt.

p. 42 I would like to . . . : "On the Endeavor of the Way," TTDE, p.

4. Lewis Richmond.

All those . . . : "The Buddhas' Teaching," TTDE, p. 279. Peter Levitt.

p. 43 Since a buddha receives . . . : "Document of Heritage," TTDE, p. 168. Lewis Richmond.

Without being . . . : "Cleansing," TTDE, p. 57. Peter Levitt.

In the authentic tradition . . . : "On the Endeavor of the Way," TTDE, p. 5. Lewis Richmond.

Just understand . . . : Ibid., p. 9.

p. 44 Since authentic transmission . . . : "The Buddhas' Teaching," TTDE, p. 278. Peter Levitt.

It is taught . . . : "On the Endeavor of the Way," TTDE, p. 18. Lewis Richmond.

When you first . . . : "Actualizing the Fundamental Point," TTDE, p. 30. Robert Aitken.

The mind that . . . : "The Mind Itself Is Buddha," TTDE, p. 46. Steve Allen.

One who has . . . : "Receiving the Marrow by Bowing," TTDE, p. 77. Peter Levitt.

When you . . . : "Document of Heritage," TTDE, p. 168. Lewis Richmond.

p. 47 Endeavor in zazen . . . : "Cypress Tree," TTDE, p. 411. Katherine Thanas.

Without practice . . . : "Body-and-Mind Study of the Way," TTDE, p. 422. Dan Welch.

The body and mind . . . : "Arousing the Aspiration for the Unsurpassable," TTDE, p. 650. Steve Allen.

The buddha way . . . : "Speaking of Mind, Speaking of Essence," TTDE, p. 497. Peter Levitt.

p. 48 Nanyue . . . : "All-Inclusive Study," TTDE, p. 610. Mel Weitsman.

Know that buddhas . . . : "Awesome Presence of Active Buddhas," TTDE, p. 260. Taigen Dan Leighton.

p. 49 Practice just here . . . : "On the Endeavor of the Way," TTDE, p. 12. Lewis Richmond.

Rujing said . . . : "Journal of My Study in China," EU, p. 27. Norman Fischer.

p. 50 [According to Ejo] . . . : "Informal Talks," EU, p. 52. Michael Wenger.

p. 52 When you ride . . . : "Actualizing the Fundamental Point," TTDE, p. 30. Robert Aitken.

p. 53 Enlightenment and clarity . . . : "Informal Talks," EU, p. 56. Michael Wenger.

To study the way . . . : "Actualizing the Fundamental Point," TTDE, p. 30. Robert Aitken.

If you attain . . . : "Confirmation," TTDE, p. 395. Lewis Richmond.

p. 54 Enlightenment is like . . . : "Actualizing the Fundamental Point," TTDE, p. 31. Robert Aitken.

All ancestors . . . : "On the Endeavor of the Way," TTDE, p. 5. Lewis Richmond.

Within this unsurpassable . . . : "Thusness," TTDE, p. 324. Mel Weitsman.

One is greatly enlightened . . . : "Great Enlightenment," TTDE, p. 297. Blanche Hartman.

p. 55 Great enlightenment . . . : Ibid., p. 300.

If you speak . . . : Ibid., p. 301.

Great enlightenment is . . . : "Continuous Practice, Part One," TTDE, p. 346. Mel Weitsman.

To carry the self . . . : "Actualizing the Fundamental Point," TTDE, p. 29. Robert Aitken.

Enlightenment is ungraspable: "Thusness," TTDE, p. 331. Mel Weitsman.

Beyond enlightenment . . . : "Continuous Practice, Part One," TTDE, p. 346. Mel Weitsman.

p. 56 On the great road . . . : Ibid., p. 332.

p. 57 There is practice-enlightenment . . . : "Actualizing the Fundamental Point," TTDE, p. 32. Robert Aitken.

One time, Huineng . . . : "Self-Realization Samadhi," TTDE, p. 695. Mel Weitsman.

Endeavors in . . . : "Mountains and Waters Sutra," TTDE, p. 159. Arnold Kotler.

The teaching of . . . : "Awesome Presence of Active Buddhas," TTDE, p. 268. Taigen Dan Leighton.

In awakening . . . : "Within a Dream Expressing the Dream," TTDE, p. 437. Taigen Dan Leighton.

p. 58 Intimacy renews . . . : "Intimate Language," TTDE, p. 535. Michael Wenger.

In a circular . . . : New translation. Peter Levitt. See also DER, p. 452.

Do not be concerned . . . : "Recommending Zazen to All People," TTDE, p. 909. Edward Brown.

Sitting in . . . : "King of Samadhis," TTDE, p. 669. Norman Fischer.

Who says . . . : "Zazen through the Seasons," BT, p. 150. Alan Senauke. See also DER, p. 369.

p. 59 Shakyamuni Buddha said . . . : "Buddha Nature," TTDE, p. 234. Mel Weitsman.

p. 60 Recognized or not . . . : "Ocean Mudra Samadhi," TTDE, p. 385. Katherine Thanas.

Know that . . . : "Buddha Nature," TTDE, p. 238. Mel Weitsman.

A monk asked . . . : Ibid., p. 255.

p. 61 As the self . . . : "Thirty-seven Wings of Enlightenment," TTDE, p. 674. Peter Levitt.

p. 62 The essential of buddha nature . . . : "Buddha Nature," TTDE, p. 241. Mel Weitsman.

Mayu . . . : "Actualizing the Fundamental Point," TTDE, p. 32. Robert Aitken.

p. 63 If you practice . . . : "On the Endeavor of the Way," TTDE, p. 21. Lewis Richmond.

p. 64 The manifestation . . . : "Manifestation of Great Prajna," TTDE, p. 25. Edward Brown.

There is the singlefold . . . : Ibid., p. 26.

I will take . . . : Ibid.

At the very moment . . . : Ibid.

p. 65 Rujing, my late master . . . : Ibid., p. 27.

To dedicate yourself . . . : Ibid., p. 28.

p. 66 Know that . . . : "Regulations for the Auxiliary Cloud Hall at the Kannondori Kosho Gokoku Monastery," TTDE, p. 39. Reb Anderson.

Your ability . . . : "Continuous Practice, Part Two," TTDE, p. 362. Mel Weitsman.

If ever . . . : Ibid., p. 365.

p. 67 Yunyan . . . : "Avalokiteshvara," TTDE, p. 397. Joan Halifax.

"Giving" means . . . : "The Bodhisattva's Four Methods of Guidance," TTDE, p. 473. Lewis Richmond.

p. 68 Know that . . . : Ibid., p. 474.

"Kind speech" . . . : Ibid., p. 495.

p. 69 Even when . . . : "Informal Talks," EU, p. 51. Michael Wenger.

"Beneficial action" . . . : "The Bodhisattva's Four Methods of Guidance," TTDE, p. 475. Lewis Richmond.

"Identity action" . . . : Ibid., p. 476.

p. 70 There are . . . : "Three Realms Are Inseparable from Mind," TTDE, p. 489. Josho Pat Phelan.

There is a simple way . . . : "Birth and Death," TTDE, p. 885. Arnold Kotler.

"Kind mind" . . . : "Instructions for the Tenzo," MD, p. 65. Arnold Kotler.

p. 71 With compassion . . . : "Guidelines for Officers of the Eihei Monastery, Echizen Province, Japan," EU, p. 245. Mel Weitsman.

[According to Ejo;] . . . : "Informal Talk," EU, p. 51. Michael Wenger.

p. 73 The realm of . . . : "On the Endeavor of the Way," TTDE, p. 8. Lewis Richmond.

When genuine . . . : Ibid.

It does not matter . . . : Ibid., p. 16.

When the Buddha was . . . : Ibid., p. 20.

p. 74 You attain . . . : "Receiving the Marrow by Bowing," TTDE, p. 72. Peter Levitt.

Generally speaking . . . : "Guidelines for Studying the Way," MD, p. 42. Dan Welch.

There is a principle . . . : "Refrain from Unwholesome Action," TTDE, p. 99. Mel Weitsman.

p. 75 Those who . . . : "Intimate Language," TTDE, p. 534. Michael Wenger.

Know that as . . . : "Buddha Sutras," TTDE, p. 541. Mel Weitsman.

Know that the root . . . : "Thirty-seven Wings of Enlightenment," TTDE, p. 678. Peter Levitt.

Those who . . . : "Guidelines for Studying the Way," MD, p. 42. Dan Welch.

p. 76 [The Buddha's] . . . : "Virtue of Home Leaving," TTDE, p. 806. Paul Haller.

[Question:] . . . : "On the Endeavor of the Way," TTDE, p. 16. Lewis Richmond.

p. 77 Having wondrous . . . : "Receiving the Marrow by Bowing," TTDE, p. 82. Peter Levitt.

Those who are . . . : Ibid., p. 79.

If you vow . . . : Ibid., p. 80.

Why are men . . . : Ibid., p. 77.

p. 78 Before becoming . . . : Ibid., p. 80.

Zhixian . . . : Ibid., p. 74.

p. 79 [After Miaoxin . . . : Ibid., p. 76

p. 80 Deshan…: "Ungraspable Mind," TTDE, p. 191. Michael Wenger.

p. 81 Even seven-year-old . . . : "Receiving the Marrow by Bowing," TTDE, p. 77. Peter Levitt.

p. 82 It is taught . . . : "Leaving the Household," TTDE, p. 766. Peter Levitt.

The entire world . . . : "The Reality of All Things," TTDE, p. 525. Lewis Richmond.

p. 83 Ancient buddhas . . . : "Refrain from Unwholesome Action," TTDE, p. 95. Mel Weitsman.

The *Guidelines* . . . : "Washing the Face," TTDE, p. 66. Linda Ruth Cutts.

p. 84 [In the ordination . . . : "Receiving the Precepts," TTDE, p. 892. Michael Wenger.

p. 86 Loving fame . . . : "Continuous Practice, Part Two," TTDE, p. 374. Mel Weitsman.

How august . . . : MD, p. 213. Brian Unger.

p. 91 You may suppose . . . : "The Time Being," TTDE, p. 108. Dan Welch.

p. 92 Do not think . . . : Ibid., p. 106.

At the time . . . : Ibid.

In essence . . . : Ibid.

Mountains are time . . . : Ibid., p. 109.

The way the self . . . : Ibid., p. 105.

The time being . . . : Ibid., p. 106.

p. 93 Spring always . . . : Ibid., p. 108.

An ancient buddha . . . : Ibid., p. 104.

p. 94 A billion worlds . . . : "Washing the Face," TTDE, p. 59. Linda Ruth Cutts.

The zazen of even . . . : "On the Endeavor of the Way," TTDE, p. 7. Lewis Richmond.

At the very moment . . . : "Cleansing," TTDE, p. 49. Peter Levitt.

[According to Senne . . . : "Zazen through the Seasons," BT, p. 144. Alan Senauke.

p. 95 A moment or two . . . : "Body-and-Mind Study of the Way," TTDE, p. 424. Dan Welch.

That which allows . . . : "Awesome Presence of Active Buddhas," TTDE, p. 264. Taigen Dan Leighton.

p. 96. Understanding these . . . : Ibid.

Hold up . . . : "Arousing the Aspiration for the Unsurpassable," TTDE, p. 650. Steve Allen.

What expounds . . . : "Space," TTDE, p. 719. Alan Senauke.

[Faxing . . . : "Turning the Dharma Wheel," TTDE, p. 692. Taigen Dan Leighton.

p. 97 Realization is . . . : "Dharma Blossoms Turn Dharma Blossoms," TTDE, p. 186. Michael Wenger.

There are those . . . : "On the Endeavor of the Way," TTDE, p. 9. Lewis Richmond.

This Saha World. . . : "Ten Directions," TTDE, p. 591. Mel Weitsman.

Even if you . . . : "Space," TTDE, p. 719. Alan Senauke.

p. 98 Know that . . . : "The Buddhas' Teaching," TTDE, p. 279. Peter Levitt.

p. 99 When you find . . . : "Actualizing the Fundamental Point," TTDE, p. 32. Robert Aitken.

The fundamental point . . . : "Great Practice," TTDE, p. 706. Dan Welch.

Only buddha ancestors . . . : "The Mind Itself Is Buddha," TTDE, p. 45. Steve Allen.

p. 100 When the self . . . : "Confirmation," TTDE, p. 391. Lewis Richmond.

The self means . . . : "Ten Directions," TTDE, p. 593. Mel Weitsman.

Speaking dharma . . . : "Insentient Beings Speak Dharma," TTDE, p. 548. Alan Senauke.

Where water . . . : "Mountains and Waters Sutra," TTDE, p. 160. Arnold Kotler.

Paramita means . . . : "The Buddhas' Teaching," TTDE, p. 282. Peter Levitt.

p. 101 All things leave . . . : "Within a Dream Expressing the Dream," TTDE, p. 432. Taigen Dan Leighton.

The zazen I speak of . . . : "Recommending Zazen to All People," TTDE, p. 907. Edward Brown.

p. 102 Snow: MD, p. 217. David Schneider. See also DER, p. 635.

Know that water . . . : "Actualizing the Fundamental Point," TTDE, p. 32. Robert Aitken.

When you see . . . : Ibid., p. 30.

p. 103 From ancient times . . . : "Mountains and Waters Sutra," TTDE, p. 163. Arnold Kotler.

There are mountains . . . : Ibid., p. 164.

The Point of Zazen: "The Point of Zazen," TTDE, p. 313. Michael Wenger and Philip Whalen.

p. 104 There is no self . . . .: "Thusness," TTDE, p. 350. Mel Weitsman.

Mind is all . . . : "The Moon," TTDE, p. 455. Mel Weitsman.

Seeing with . . . : "All-Inclusive Study," TTDE, p. 610. Mel Weitsman.

p. 105 As all things . . . : "Actualizing the Fundamental Point," TTDE, p. 29. Robert Aitken.

When you paint . . . : "Plum Blossoms," TTDE, p. 588. Mel Weitsman.

p. 106 With the body . . . : "Arousing the Aspiration for Enlightenment," TTDE, p. 659. Steve Allen.

Do you attain . . . : "Informal Talks," BT, p. 10. Michael Wenger.

p. 107 Thusness is . . . : "Arousing the Aspiration for the Unsurpassable," TTDE, p. 651. Steve Allen.

Since buddha . . . : "Continuous Practice, Part Two," TTDE, p. 379. Mel Weitsman.

For the time being . . . : "Body-and-Mind Study of the Way," TTDE, p. 422. Dan Welch.

p. 108 Moment by moment . . . : "Power of the Robe," TTDE, p. 117. Blanche Hartman.

Cleansing body and mind . . . : "Washing the Face," TTDE, p. 58. Linda Ruth Cutts.

In zazen . . . : "On the Endeavor of the Way," TTDE, p. 6. Lewis Richmond.

p. 109 At the very . . . : "King of Samadhis," TTDE, p. 667. Norman Fischer.

p. 110 Huineng . . . : "Continuous Practice, Part One," TTDE, p. 328. Mel Weitsman.

Great Master Shakyamuni . . . : "Three Realms Are Inseparable from Mind," TTDE, p. 487. Josho Pat Phelan.

p. 111 Mind is skin. . .: Ibid., p. 490.

The practice of . . . : "On the Endeavor of the Way," TTDE, p. 12. Lewis Richmond.

Mountains, rivers . . . : "The Mind Itself Is Buddha," TTDE, p. 46. Steve Allen.

Everyday mind is the way . . . : "Buddha Nature," TTDE, p. 235. Mel Weitsman.

p. 112 When studying . . . : "Continuous Practice, Part One," TTDE, p. 340. Mel Weitsman.

On Nondependence . . . : MD, p. 214. Brian Unger.

p. 113 The great way . . . : "Undivided Activity," TTDE, p. 450. Edward Brown.

p. 114 You should . . .: "On the Endeavor of the Way," TTDE, p. 15. Lewis Richmond.

Know that . . . : "Awesome Presence of the Buddhas," TTDE, p. 265. Taigen Dan Leighton.

Shenshan . . . : "Speaking of Mind, Speaking of Essence," TTDE, p. 493. Peter Levitt.

Birth is just like . . . : "Undivided Activity," TTDE, p. 451. Edward Brown.

p. 115 The Buddha said . . . : "Arousing the Aspiration for Enlightenment," TTDE, p. 660. Steve Allen.

In regard to . . . : "Awesome Presence of Active Buddhas," TTDE, p. 268. Taigen Dan Leighton.

p. 116 Within the cycles . . . : "Continuous Practice, Part One," TTDE, p. 347. Mel Weitsman.

Although there is . . . : "Birth and Death," TTDE, p. 885. Arnold Kotler.

In birth there is . . . : Ibid.

Firewood . . . : "Actualizing the Fundamental Point," TTDE, p. 30. Robert Aitken.

p. 117 Given to . . . : EU, p. 206. Jane Hirshfield.

p. 118 The real issue . . . : "Refrain from Unwholesome Action," TTDE, p. 103. Mel Weitsman.

Cause is . . . : Ibid., p. 100.

From the present . . . : "Arousing the Aspiration for Enlightenment," TTDE, p. 659. Steve Allen.

p. 119 The World-Honored One . . . : "Karma in the Three Periods," TTDE, p. 790. Mel Weitsman.

There are no exceptions . . . : "Identifying with Cause and Effect," TTDE, p. 857. Katherine Thanas.

Baizhang . . . : "Great Practice," TTDE, p. 705. Dan Welch.

p. 120 The most serious . . . : "Identifying with Cause and Effect," TTDE, p. 853. Katherine Thanas.

Immediately clarify . . . : Ibid., p. 857.

Reflect quietly . . . : "Washing the Face," TTDE, p. 69. Linda Ruth Cutts.

Ignoring causation . . . : "Identifying with Cause and Effect," TTDE, p. 855. Katherine Thanas.

Venerable Kumaralabha . . . : "Karma in the Three Periods," TTDE, p. 779. Mel Weitsman.

p. 121 What Kumaralabha meant . . . : Ibid., p. 780.

p. 122 [Keizan Jokin . . . : "Dogen's Life and Teaching," TTDE, p. 911. Susan Moon.

p. 123 The concentrated endeavor of the way . . . : "On the Endeavor of the Way," TTDE, p. 3. Lewis Richmond.

All-inclusive study . . . : "All-Inclusive Study," TTDE, p. 614. Mel Weitsman.

In stillness . . . : "On the Endeavor of the Way," TTDE, p. 36. Lewis Richmond.

The embodiment . . . : "The Point of Zazen," TTDE, p. 304. Michael Wenger.

p. 124 "Freedom" means . . . : "Arhat," TTDE, p. 404. Peter Levitt.

Enlightenment disappears . . . : "Great Enlightenment," TTDE, p. 296. Blanche Hartman.

One day while . . . : "Valley Sounds, Mountain Colors," TTDE, p. 87. Katherine Thanas.

p. 125 Know that . . . : "Turning the Dharma Wheel," TTDE, p. 693. Taigen Dan Leighton.

When you leap . . . : "Reading a Sutra," TTDE, p. 224. John Daido Loori.

p. 126 Original Face: EU, p. 256. Brian Unger.

When you turn . . . : "Arousing the Aspiration for the Unsurpassable," TTDE, p. 652. Steve Allen.

p. 127 Saying that . . . : "Valley Sounds, Mountain Colors," TTDE, p. 89. Katherine Thanas.

All buddhas . . . : "Within a Dream Expressing the Dream," TTDE, p. 432. Taigen Dan Leighton.

Because mountains . . . : "Mountains and Waters Sutra," TTDE, p. 154. Arnold Kotler.

Because earth . . . : "On the Endeavor of the Way," TTDE, p. 6. Lewis Richmond.

Although there are many . . . : "Actualizing the Fundamental Point," TTDE, p. 31. Robert Aitken.

p. 128 In Song China . . . : "Valley Sounds, Mountain Colors,"
TTDE, p. 85. Katherine Thanas.

Are mountain colors . . . : Ibid., p. 86.

One spring . . . : Ibid., p. 88.

p. 129 Mountains and waters . . . : "Mountains and Waters Sutra,"
TTDE, p. 154. Arnold Kotler.

Mountains' walking . . . : Ibid.

All waters appear . . . : Ibid., p. 158.

An ancient buddha . . . : "Only a Buddha and a Buddha," TTDE, p.
880. Edward Brown.

p. 130 When the time . . . : "Flowers in the Sky," TTDE, p. 462.
Dan Welch.

When the old plum . . . : "Plum Blossoms," TTDE, p. 582. Mel
Weitsman.

To follow ancient . . . : "Guidelines for Officers of the Eihei
Monastery," EU, p. 234. Mel Weitsman.

p. 131 The coming . . . : "The Mind Itself Is Buddha," TTDE, p.
46. Steve Allen.

Both blossoms... : "Flowers in the Sky," TTDE, p. 459. Dan Welch.

Know that . . . : "The Moon," TTDE, p. 457. Mel Weitsman.

p. 133 The miracles . . . : "Miracles," TTDE, p. 287. Katherine
Thanas.

Miracles arise . . . : Ibid.

Guishan is . . . : Ibid.

p. 134 Encompassed by . . . : Ibid., p. 289.

p. 135 The teaching, practice . . . : Ibid.

Layman Pangyun . . . : Ibid., p. 290.

p. 136 Causing water . . . : Ibid., p. 291.

The miracles transmitted . . . : Ibid., p. 294.

The buddha dharma . . . : Ibid., p. 295.

p. 139 In the practice . . . : "Receiving the Marrow by Bowing,"
TTDE, p. 72. Peter Levitt.

Endeavor wholeheartedly . . . : "Valley Sounds, Mountain Colors,"
TTDE, p. 93. Katherine Thanas.

p. 140 In response to . . . : "Arousing the Aspiration for Enlightenment," TTDE, p. 656. Steve Allen.

Just understand . . . : "On the Endeavor of the Way," TTDE, p. 9. Lewis Richmond.

When Shakyamuni . . . : "Seeing the Buddha," TTDE, p. 598. Gaelyn Godwin.

I recommend . . . : "On the Endeavor of the Way," TTDE, p. 13. Lewis Richmond.

Don't scold or criticize . . . : "Informal Talks," EU, p. 50. Michael Wenger.

p. 141 When you penetrate . . . : "Twining Vines," TTDE, p. 482. Mel Weitsman.

p. 142 As he was . . . : "Thusness," TTDE, p. 330. Mel Weitsman.

In Honor of . . . : EU, p. 199. Jane Hirshfield.

[According to Ejo . . . : "Formal Talks," BT, p. 144. Alan Senauke. See also DER, p. 164.

p. 144 When the Buddha . . . : "Taking Refuge in Buddha, Dharma, and Sangha," TTDE, p. 847. Gyokuko Carlson and Kyogen Carlson.

Question . . . : "On the Endeavor of the Way," TTDE, p.16. Lewis Richmond.

p. 145 Lay bodhisattvas . . . : "Power of the Robe," TTDE, p. 129. Blanche Hartman.

I rejoice . . . : Ibid., p. 135.

Those who are called . . . : "Receiving the Marrow by Bowing," TTDE, p. 77. Peter Levitt.

Buddha ancestors . . . : "On the Endeavor of the Way," TTDE, p.16. Lewis Richmond.

p. 147 Those who have not . . . : "Thirty-Seven Wings of Enlightenment," TTDE, p. 682. Peter Levitt.

p. 148 All buddha . . . : "On the Endeavor of the Way," TTDE, p. 3. Lewis Richmond.

Transmission of . . . : "The Point of Zazen," TTDE, p. 309. Michael Wenger.

A face-to-face-transmitting . . . : "Face-to-Face Transmission," TTDE, p. 571. Reb Anderson.

p. 149 I first offered . . . : Ibid., p. 569.

The great master . . . : "On the Endeavor of the Way," TTDE, p. 7. Lewis Richmond.

Shakyamuni Buddha once . . . : "Document of Heritage," TTDE, p. 170. Lewis Richmond.

p. 150 The meaning of . . . : Ibid.

From Shakyamuni . . . : "The Buddha Way," TTDE, p. 501. Mel Weitsman.

p. 151 When Linji was . . . : Ibid., p. 511.

p. 152 Continuous practice that . . . : "Continuous Practice, Part One," TTDE, p. 333. Mel Weitsman.

Blossoms opening . . . : Ibid.

Great Teacher . . . : Ibid., p. 334.

p. 153 From the time . . . : Ibid., p. 338.

The continuous practice . . . : Ibid., p. 345.

p. 154 In the continuous practice . . . : Ibid.

If you attain . . . : Ibid., p. 347.

Continuous practice, day . . . : "Continuous Practice, Part Two," TTDE, p. 365. Mel Weitsman.

Do not run . . . : Ibid., p. 379.

Zhaozhou . . . : "Continuous Practice, Part One," TTDE, p. 339. Mel Weitsman.

p. 155 Monks' actions . . . : "Thirty-seven Wings of Enlightenment," TTDE, p. 689. Peter Levitt.

p. 159 When you encounter . . . : "Intimate Language," TTDE, p. 535. Michael Wenger.

p. 160 Priest Daokai . . . : "Everyday Activity," TTDE, p. 621. Katherine Thanas.

Yunju . . . : "Intimate Language," TTDE, p. 531. Michael Wenger.

p. 161 An old buddha . . . : "Awesome Presence of Active Buddhas," TTDE, p. 263. Taigen Dan Leighton.

p. 162 Know that the World-Honored One . . . : "Four Horses," TTDE, p. 793. Peter Levitt.

The World-Honored One . . . : "Intimate Language," TTDE, p. 534. Michael Wenger.

Zhaozhou...: "Everyday Activity," TTDE, p. 625. Katherine Thanas.

p. 163 When you . . . : "Expressions," TTDE, p. 442. Peter Levitt.

A number of . . . : "Thirty-Seven Wings of Enlightenment," TTDE, p. 688. Peter Levitt.

p. 164 Bodhisattvas who . . . : "Valley Sounds, Mountain Colors," TTDE, p. 86. Katherine Thanas.

Water is not just . . . : "Mountains and Waters Sutra," TTDE, p. 159. Arnold Kotler.

Because green . . . : Ibid., p. 155.

If you doubt . . . : Ibid.

p. 165 Walking forward . . . : Ibid.

There is walking . . . : Ibid., p. 156.

A billion worlds . . . : "Body-and-Mind Study of the Way," TTDE, p. 423. Dan Welch.

There is no . . . : "Painting of a Rice Cake," TTDE, p. 448. Dan Welch.

Taking up . . . : "Flowers in the Sky," TTDE, p. 460. Dan Welch.

p. 166 The Tathagata says . . . : Ibid., p. 456.

Go away with . . . : "The Point of Zazen," TTDE, p. 313. Michael Wenger.

When the sky . . . : Ibid.

The vast sky . . . : "Going Beyond Buddha," TTDE, p. 321. Mel Weitsman.

Here is one . . . : "Thusness," TTDE, p. 326. Mel Weitsman.

The withered tree . . . : "Dragon Song," TTDE, p. 627. Mel Weitsman.

p. 167 A tree with . . . : "Within a Dream Expressing the Dream," TTDE, p. 433. Taigen Dan Leighton.

Know that . . . : "Awesome Presence of Active Buddhas," TTDE, p. 274. Taigen Dan Leighton.

The Body Born . . . : MD, p. 214. Brian Unger.

p. 168 Closing the Furnace . . . : "Zazen through the Seasons," BT, p. 148. Alan Senauke. See also DER, p. 435.

A plantain has earth . . . : "Painting of a Rice Cake," TTDE, p. 448. Dan Welch.

The paints for painting . . . : Ibid., p. 445.

At the moment of attaining . . . : Ibid. p. 447.

When a buddha is . . . : Ibid., p. 446.

p. 169 Shigong . . . : "Space," TTDE, p. 717. Alan Senauke; Peter Levitt (verse commentary, new translation). See also TDE, p. 340.

p. 170 Dongshan . . . : "Insentient Beings Speak Dharma," TTDE, p. 552. Alan Senauke; Peter Levitt (verse commentary, new translation). See also TDE, p. 200.

Once, Caoshan . . . : Peter Levitt, new translation. See also TDE, p. 355.

p. 172 Given to . . . : Ibid. See also DER, p. 624.

Response to Graduate . . . : Ibid. See also DER, p. 610.

p. 173 Given to Imperial . . . : Ibid. See also DER, p. 619.

Given to Chengzhong: Ibid. See also DER, p. 617.

Given to Sukemitsu . . . : Ibid. See also DER, p. 625.

During Retreat. Intimate . . . : Ibid. See also DER, p. 627.

p. 174 During Retreat. Last night . . . : Ibid. See also DER, p. 626.

Secluded in the Mountains. How pathetic . . . : Ibid. See also DER, p. 640.

Secluded in the Mountains. The evening . . . : Ibid. See also DER, p 641.

Secluded in the Mountains. The ancestor's . . . : MD, p. 216. David Schneider. See also DER, p. 638.

p. 175 Snow and more . . . : BT, p. 145. Alan Senauke. See also DER, p. 351.

Buddha's Enlightenment: MD, p. 216. David Schneider. See also DER, p. 637.

Death Poem: MD, p. 219. Philip Whalen.

p. 176 Splattering salt . . . : Peter Levitt, new translation. See also DER, p. 606.

p. 177 Sun face . . . : Ibid. See also DER, p. 604.

For thousands . . . : MD, p. 216. David Schneider. See also DER, p. 608.

This autumn . . . : Peter Levitt, new translation. See also DER, p. 602.

If you call . . . : Ibid. See also DER, p. 605.

Chronology of Dogen's Life

Dates are shown in the order of year, month, and day (if known); e.g., "4-9" below "1213" means the ninth day of the fourth month in the lunar calendar. The chronology of Dogen's texts follows that of traditional scholarship in case the month or day of their emergence is not known.

See the "Editors' Notes to the Reader" regarding the East Asian calendar system and our use of macrons.

Dogen at times referred to the Kosho Horin Monastery and other places where he taught in various ways, which are reflected in our descriptions of events in this chapter.

———————————————

EARLY PERIOD
1200
Born in Kyōto.

1207
Mother passes away.

1212
Spring   Visits monk Ryōkan at the foot of Mount Hiei with a wish to be a monk. Then enters Shuryōgon Temple. Later moves to Senkō Temple.

1213

4-9 Head shaved by Kōen, principal priest of Tendai School.

4-10 Receives monk precepts at the Precept Hall, Enryaku Monastery, Mount Hiei.

1214

Spring   Visits Kōin of Onjō Monastery and asks about essentials of dharma. Later, meets Eisai.

1217

8-25 Enters Kennin Monastery, Kyōto, and starts practicing with Myōzen.

1221

9-22 Receives a certificate of completion of study (inka) from Myōzen.

1223

2-22 Leaves Kennin Monastery with Myōzen on a journey to China.

4 Arrives at Qingyuan Port, Zhejiang, China.

5-4 While on board, meets head cook of Ayuwang Monastery.

7 Enters Tiantong Jingde Monastery and sees Wuji Liaopai.

Autumn   Sees a document of heritage of Longmen Fayan lineage.

1224

1-21 Sees a document of heritage of Wuji Liaopai lineage.

Winter   Starts a pilgrimage to monasteries in Zhejiang Province.

1225

Spring   Meets Zhuoweng Ruyan of Mount Jia. Later, meets Yuanzi of Wannian Monastery, Pingtian, and sees a document of heritage. Studies with Panshan Saizhuo of Xiaocuicui, Tai Region. Visits Husheng Monastery, Mount Damei.

5-1 Meets Tiantong Rujing and receives dharma transmission.

5-21 Myōzen passes away at Tiantong Jingde Monastery.

Summer   Visits Ayuwang Monastery again.

7-2 Enters Rujing's quarters for the first time.

During the summer practice period, realizes the great matter upon hearing Rujing speaking of "dropping away body and mind."

9-18 Receives bodhisattva precepts from Rujing.

1226

Visits Putuoshan Island

1227

7 Receives document of heritage from Rujing.

7 Leaves Tiantong Jingde Monastery.

7 Leaves Qingyuan Port. Arrives at Kawajiri, Higo Province, Kyūshū.

WANDERING PERIOD

1227

Enters Kennin Monastery, Kyōto.

7-15 Completes "Recommending Zazen to All People" (Fukan Zazen Gi).

10-5 Completes "Record of Bringing Master Myōzen's Relics" (Shari Sōden Ki).

1231

Spring   Moves to An'yō Temple in Fukakusa, a village to the south of Kyōto.

7 Expounds dharma to Nun Ryōnen.

8-15 Completes "On the Endeavor of the Way" (Bendowa).

KŌSHŌ MONASTERY PERIOD

1233

Spring   Opens Kannon-dōri Kōshō Hōrin Monastery upon request of Noriie Fujiwara and Nun Shōgaku.

4-15 Starts a summer practice period.

On a day of the summer practice period, presents "Manifestation of Great Prajñā" (Maka Hannya Haramitsu), *Treasury of the True Dharma Eye* (TTDE—Shōbō Genzō).

7-15 Ends the summer practice period. (From this year on, holds a summer practice period annually on the same dates, with the possible exception of 1244.)

8 Gives "Actualizing the Fundamental Point" (Genjō Kōan), TTDE, to Kōshū Yō.

1234

3-9 Expounds "Guidelines for Studying the Way" (Gakudō Yōjin Shū).

Winter Ejō joins Dōgen's temporary monastery. Soon he starts transcribing Dōgen's informal evening talks, to be collected in the *Treasury of the True Dharma Eye: Things I Heard* (Shōbō Genzō Zuimon Ki).

1235

8-15 Gives Ejō bodhisattva precepts.

12 Writes "Donation Request for a Monks' Hall at the Kannondōri Monastery" (Kannon-dōri In Sōdō Konryū Kanjin So).

This year, makes a collection of three hundred Chinese Zen kōans, to be known as *Chinese Language Treasury of the True Dharma Eye* (Shinji Shōbō Genzō).

1236

10-15 Opens the monks' hall at the monastery. Renames his practice center Kōshō (Raising Sages) Zen Monastery.

12-28 Appoints Ejō head monk.

1237

Spring   Completes "Instructions for the Tenzo" (Tenzo Kyōkun)

This year, completes "Guideline for Monk Ordination" (Shukke Jukai Sahō).

1238

4-18 Presents "One Bright Pearl" (Ikka Myōju), TTDE.

1239

4-25 Completes "Regulations for the Auxiliary Cloud Hall at the Kannon-dōri Kōshō Gokoku Monastery" (Kannondōri Kōshō Gokoku-ji Jū'un-dō Shiki).

5-25 Presents "The Mind Itself Is Buddha" (Sokushin Zebutsu), TTDE.

10-23 Presents "Cleansing" (Senjō), TTDE.

10-23 Presents "Washing the Face" (Semmen), TTDE.

1240

The fifteenth day after spring solstice, completes "Receiving the Marrow by Bowing" (Raihai Tokuzui), TTDE.

4-19 Presents "Valley Sounds, Mountain Colors" (Keisei Sanshoku), TTDE.

8-15 Presents "Refrain from Unwholesome Action" (Shoaku Makusa), TTDE.

10-1 Completes "The Time Being" (Uji), TTDE.

10-1 Presents "Power of the Robe" (Kesa Kudoku), TTDE.

10-1 Completes "Transmitting the Robe" (Den'e), TTDE.

10-18 Presents "Mountains and Waters Sūtra" (Sansuikyō), TTDE.

1241

1-3 Presents "Buddha Ancestors" (Busso), TTDE.

3-27 Completes "Document of Heritage" (Shisho), TTDE.

Spring   Completes "Afterword for the *Recorded Sayings of Zen Master Tiantong Rujing*, Sequel" (Tendō Nyojō Zenji Zoku Goroku).

Spring   Students of Kakuan of Daruma School, including Ekan, Gikai, Giin, Gien, and Gijun, join Dōgen's community.

During the summer practice period, gives "Dharma Blossoms Turn Dharma Blossoms" (Hokke Ten Hokke), TTDE, to Etatsu.

During the summer practice period, presents "Ungraspable Mind" (Shin Fukatoku), TTDE.

During the summer practice period, completes "Ungraspable Mind, Later Version" (Go Shin Fukatoku), TTDE.

9-9 Presents "Old Mirror" (Kokyō), TTDE.

9-15 Presents "Reading a Sūtra" (Kankin), TTDE.

10-14 Presents "Buddha Nature" (Busshō), TTDE.

10 Completes "Awesome Presence of Active Buddhas" (Gyōbutsu Iigi), TTDE.

11-14 Presents "The Buddhas' Teaching" (Bukkyō), TTDE.

11-16 Presents "Miracles" (Jinzū), TTDE.

1242

1-28 Presents "Great Enlightenment" (Daigo), TTDE.

3-18 Completes "The Point of Zazen" (Zazen Shin), TTDE.

3-23 Presents "Going Beyond Buddha" (Bukkōjō Ji), TTDE.

3-26 Presents "Thusness" (Immo), TTDE.

4-5 Completes "Continuous Practice" (Gyōji), TTDE.

4-20 Completes "Ocean Mūdra Samadhi" (Kai'in Zemmai), TTDE.

4-25 Completes "Confirmation," (Juki), TTDE.

4-26 Presents "Avalokiteshvara" (Kannon), TTDE.

5-15 Presents "Arhat" (Arakan), TTDE.

5-21 Presents "Cypress Tree" (Hakujushi), TTDE.

6-2 Presents "Radiant Light" (Kōmyō), TTDE.

9-9 Presents "Body-and-Mind Study of the Way" (Shinjin Gakudō), TTDE.

9-21 Presents "Within a Dream Expressing the Dream" (Muchū Setsumu), TTDE.

10-5 Completes "Expressions" (Dōtoku), TTDE.

11-5 Presents "Painting of a Rice Cake" (Gabyō), TTDE.

12-17 Presents "Undivided Activity" (Zenki), TTDE, at the Kyōto residence of Yoshishige Hatano.

This year, gives bodhisattva precepts to Kakushin of Saihō Monastery.

1243

1-6 Completes "The Moon" (Tsuki), TTDE.

3-10 Presents "Flowers in the Sky" (Kūge), TTDE.

4-29 Presents "Old Buddha Mind" (Kobutsu Shin), TTDE, at Rokuharamitsu Temple in Kyōto.

5-5 Completes "Bodhisattva's Four Methods of Guidance" (Bodaisatta Shi Shōhō), TTDE.

7-7 Presents "Twining Vines" (Kattō), TTDE.

7-15 Ends the summer practice period.

7 Dōgen and most of his community move to Echizen Province.

MONASTERY CONSTRUCTION PERIOD

1243

1-28 Presents "Great Enlightenment" (Daigo), TTDE, for the second time.

7-17 Yoshishige Hatano and Layman Sakingo (Kakunen) find land suitable for Dōgen's monastery, in Shihi, Echizen Province.

Intercalary 7-1, presents "Three Realms Are Inseparable from Mind" (Sangai Yuishin), TTDE, to the assembly on Mount Yoshimine.

This year, presents "Speaking of Mind, Speaking of Essence" (Sesshin Sesshō), TTDE, to the assembly of Yoshimine Temple.

9-16 Presents "The Buddha Way" (Butsudō), TTDE, to the assembly of Yoshimine Temple.

9 Presents "The Reality of All Things" (Shohō Jissō), TTDE, to the assembly of Yoshimine Temple.

9-20 Presents "Intimate Language" (Mitsugo), TTDE, to the assembly of Yoshimine Temple.

9 Presents "Buddha Sūtras" (Bukkyō), TTDE, to the assembly of Yoshimine Temple.

10-2 Presents "Insentient Beings Speak Dharma" (Mujō Seppō), TTDE, to the assembly of Yoshimine Temple.

10 Presents "Dharma Nature" (Hosshō), TTDE, to the assembly of Yoshimine Temple.

This year, presents "Dharani" (Darani), TTDE, to the assembly of Yoshimine Temple.

10-20 Presents "Face-to-Face Transmission" (Menju), TTDE, to the assembly of Yoshimine Temple.

10-20 Presents "Washing the Face" (Semmen), TTDE, for the second time.

11 Presents "Rules for Zazen" (Zazen Gi), TTDE, to the assembly of Yoshimine Temple.

11-6 Completes "Plum Blossoms" (Baika), TTDE, at Yoshimine Temple.

11-13 Presents "Ten Directions" (Jippō), TTDE, to the assembly of Yoshimine Temple.

11-19 Presents "Seeing the Buddha" (Kembutsu), TTDE, to the assembly at Yamashi Peak.

11-27 Presents "All-Inclusive Study" (Henzan), TTDE, in a grass-thatched hut at the foot of Yamashi Peak.

12-17 Presents "Eyeball" (Ganzei), TTDE, to the assembly at Yamashi Peak.

12-17 Presents "Everyday Activity" (Kajō), TTDE, to the assembly at the foot of Yamashi Peak.

12-25 Presents "Dragon Song" (Ryūgin), TTDE, to the assembly on the foot of Yamashi Peak.

1244

2-4 Presents "The Meaning of Bodhidharma's Coming from India" (Soshi Sairai I), TTDE, to the assembly in a deep mountain of Echizen.

2-12 Presents "Udumbara Blossom" (Udonge), TTDE, to the assembly of Yoshimine Temple.

2-14 Presents "Arousing the Aspiration for the Unsurpassable" (Hotsu Mujō Shin), TTDE, to the assembly of Yoshimine Temple.

2-14 Presents "Arousing the Aspiration for Enlightenment" (Hotsu Bodai Shin), TTDE, to the assembly of Yoshimine Temple.

2-15 Presents "Tathāgata's Entire Body" (Nyorai Zenshin), TTDE, to the assembly of Yoshimine Temple.

2-15 Presents "King of Samādhis" (Sammai Ōzammai), TTDE, to the assembly of Yoshimine Temple.

2-21 Foundation stones for the new monastery are set and the pillars are erected.

Presents "Guidelines for Interacting with Great Five-Summer (Senior) Teachers (Tai Daiko Goke Jari Hō)."

2-22 The wooden framework of the dharma hall is raised.

2-24 Presents "Thirty-Seven Wings of Enlightenment" (Sanjūshichi Hon Bodai Bumpō), TTDE, to the assembly of Yoshimine Temple.

2-27 Presents "Turning the Dharma Wheel" (Tembōrin), TTDE, to the assembly of Yoshimine Temple.

2-29 Presents "Self-Realization Samadhi" (Jishō Zammai), TTDE, to the assembly of Yoshimine Temple.

3-9 Presents "Great Practice" (Dai Shugyō), TTDE, to the assembly of Yoshimine Temple.

This year, presents "Spring and Autumn" (Shunjū), TTDE, to the assembly in a deep mountain of Echizen.

DAIBUTSU MONASTERY PERIOD

1244

7-18 Moves from Yoshimine Temple to his new monastery. Opens its dharma hall and names it Daibutsu (Great Buddha) Monastery.

8-14 Makes a vow to hand carve a Buddha image for the monastery.

9-1 Performs a ceremony marking completion of the dharma hall.

11-3 Performs a framework-raising ceremony for the monks' hall.

This year, appoints Gikai tenzo.

1245

3-6 Presents "Space" (Kokū), TTDE.

3-12 Presents "Eating Bowl" (Hou), TTDE.

5 Gives dharma words to Hironaga Hatano.

6-13 Presents "Practice Period" (Ango), TTDE.

7-4 Presents "Seeing Others' Minds" (Tashin Tsū), TTDE.

9-25 Writes a waka on the first snowfall of the year.

10-22 Presents "King Wants the Saindhava" (Ōsaku Sendaba), TTDE.

EIHEI MONASTERY PERIOD

1246

3 Tokiyori Hōjō becomes the fifth regent of the Kamakura government and invites Dōgen to Kamakura.

6-15 Renames his training monastery, Eihei (Eternal Peace) Monastery.

6-15 Completes "Guidelines for Officers of the Eihei Monastery, Echizen Province, Japan" (Nihon Koku Echizen Eihei-ji Chiji Shingi).

8-6 Presents "Instructions on Kitchen Work" (Ji Kuin Mon).

9-6 Presents "Leaving the Household" (Shukke), TTDE.

1247

1 Writes "Auspicious Beginning of Spring" (Risshun Daikichi Mon).

1-15 Conducts a repentance ceremony.

Summer   Appoints Gikai director of Eihei Monastery.

8-3 Leaves for Kamakura to teach laypeople, primarily leaders of the samurai government.

This year, gives precepts to a number of people, including Tokiyori Hōjō. Gives him ten waka poems.

1248

2-14 Drafts a dharma talk on the six ministers of King Ajātashatru at a layperson's residence near Kamakura.

3-13 Returns to Eihei Monastery, ready to lead the practice period.

3-14 Gives a formal dharma talk.

11-1 Renames Sanshō Peak behind the monastery Mount Kisshō.

12-21 Completes "Five Guidelines for the Kitchen at Eihei Monastery" (Eihei-ji Kuin Seiki Go-kajō).

1249
Completes "Guidelines for the Study Hall at the Kisshō Mountain, Eihei Monastery" (Kisshō-zan Eihei-ji Shuryō Shingi).
8 Adds a poem to a portrait of him viewing the moon.
10 Writes "Nine Reminders for Residents of Eihei Monastery" (Eihei-ji Jūryo Kokoroe Ku-kajō).

1250
1-11 Presents "Washing the Face" (Semmen), TTDE, for the third time.

1251
1-5 Discusses dharma with Minister Hanayama in a hut at Ryōzen Temple in Shihi Village.

1252
This year, revises "Actualizing the Fundamental Point" (Genjō Kōan), TTDE.
Autumn   Becomes ill.

1253
1-6 Expounds the *Pari-nirvāna Admonition Outline Sūtra*.
1-6 Completes "Eight Awakenings of Great Beings" (Hachi Dainin Gaku), TTDE.
4-27 Asks Gikai about the passing of his former teacher Ekan in a hut at Ryōzen Temple in Shihi Village.
7-8 Becomes ill again. Gikai attends to him.
7-14 Appoints Ejō the second abbot of Eihei Monastery, giving him a personally sewn robe.

8-5 Leaves for Kyōto for medical treatment.

8-15 Under a harvest moon, writes a poem:

> In autumn
> even though I may
> see it again,
> how can I sleep
> with the moon this evening?

8-28 Passes away at his lay student Kakunen's residence in Kyōto.

Selected Bibliography

Bein, Steve, trans. *Purifying Zen: Watsuji Tesuro's* "Shamon Dogen."
   Honolulu: University of Hawai'i Press, 2011.
Bielefeldt, Carl. *Dogen's Manuals of Zen Meditation*. Berkeley:
   University of California Press, 1988.
Bokusan Nishiari, Shohaku Okumura, Shunryu Suzuki, Kosho
   Uchiyama, Sojun Mel Weitsman, Kazuaki Tanahashi, Dairyu
   Michael Wenger, commentary and trans. *Dogen's Genjo Koan:
   Three Commentaries*. Berkeley: Counterpoint, 2011.
Cleary, Thomas, trans. *Record of Things Heard: The Shobogenzo
   Zuimonki, Talks of Zen Master Dogen as Recorded by Zen Master
   Ejo*. Boulder, Colo.: Prajna Press, 1980.
Heine, Steven. *Did Dogen Go to China?: What He Wrote and When He
   Wrote It*. New York: Oxford University Press, 2006.
———. *Dogen and the Koan Tradition: A Tale of Two Shobogenzo
   Texts*. Albany: State University of New York Press, 1994.
———. *The Zen Poetry of Dogen: Verses from the Mountain of Eternal
   Peace*. Boston: Tuttle Publishing, 1997.
Kodera, Takashi James. *Dogen's Formative Years in China: An
   Historical Study and Annotated Translation of the Hokyo-ki*. Boulder,
   Colo.: Prajna Press, 1980.
Leighton, Taigen Dan. *Visions of Awakening Space and Time: Dogen
   and the Lotus Sutra*. New York: Oxford University Press, 2007.

————. *Zen Questions: Zazen, Dogen, and the Spirit of Creative Inquiry*. Boston: Wisdom Publications, 2011.

Leighton, Taigen Dan, and Shohaku Okumura, trans. *Dogen's Extensive Record: A Translation of the Eihei Koroku*. Boston: Wisdom Publications, 2004.

————, trans. *Dogen's Pure Standards for the Zen Community: A Translation of Eihei Shingi*. Albany: State University of New York Press, 1996.

Nishijima, Gudo Wafu, and Chodo Cross, trans. *Master Dogen's Shobogenzo*. 4 vols. Woods Hole, Mass.: Windbell Publications, 1994–1998.

Okumura, Shohaku, trans. and ed. *Dogen Zen*. Kyoto: Kyoto Soto Zen Center, 1988.

————, trans. *Shobogenzo Zuimonki: Sayings of Eihei Dogen Zenji, Recorded by Koun Ejo*. Kyoto: Kyoto Soto Zen Center, 1987.

————. *Realizing Genjokoan: The Key to Dogen's "Shobogenzo."* Boston: Wisdom Publications, 2010.

Okumura, Shohaku, and Taigen Dan Leighton, trans. *The Wholehearted Way: A Translation of Eihei Dogen's Bendowa with Commentary by Kosho Uchiyama Roshi*. Boston: Charles Tuttle, 1997.

Tanahashi, Kazuaki, ed. and trans. *Beyond Thinking: A Guide to Zen Meditation; Zen Master Dogen*. Boston: Shambhala Publications, 2004.

————. *Enlightenment Unfolds: The Essential Teachings of Zen Master Dogen*. Boston: Shambhala Publications, 1999.

————. *Moon in a Dewdrop: Writings of Zen Master Dogen*. New York: North Point Press, 1985.

————, ed. *Treasury of the True Dharma Eye: Zen Master Dogen's Shobo Genzo*. Boston: Shambhala Publications, 2010.

Tanahashi, Kazuaki, and John Daido Loori, trans., with commentary and verse by John Daido Loori. *The True Dharma Eye: Zen Master Dogen's Three Hundred Koans*. Boston: Shambhala Publications, 2005.

Verkuilen, Barbara. *Dokusan with Dogen: Timeless Lessons in Negotiating the Way*. Madison, Wis.: Firethroat Press, 2011.

Waddell, Norman, and Abe Masao, trans. *The Heart of Dogen's "Shobogenzo."* Albany, State University of New York Press, 2002.

Warner, Brad. *Sit Down and Shut Up: Punk Rock Commentaries on Buddha, God, Truth, Sex, Death, and Dogen's Treasury of the Right Dharma Eye*. Novato, Calif.: New World Library, 2007.